# RITES
and
# RITUALS

## HARNESSING THE POWER
## OF SACRED CEREMONY

# AHRIANA PLATTEN, PH.D

FEATURING: REV. ASHERAH ALLEN, DR. AVEEN BANICH,
ROGER BUTTS, MAEVEN ELLER-FIVE, LIZ GOLL LERNER, TINA GREEN,
ERICA JONES, JANA ROSELYNN LAIRD, REV. SHENNA LEE-BELMORE,
REV. MARY ROSE LOVE, KELLI MURBACH, JEN PICENO,
REV. MARK J. PLATTEN, JANICE PRATT, MILAGROS RUIZ BELLO,
MISTY DAWN SHAKTI SHARMA, HEATHER SOUTHARD,
KAT SPARKS, SUSAN M THOMPSON, REV. JESSICA TROVIK

# A FEW WORDS FROM OUR COVER ARTIST

### SAMUEL FARRAND
### TITLE: *APEX II*

Each work I create contains the presence of Duality (Void & Light), which, when the two are in harmony with one another, become Singular. Collectively, each design demonstrates a unique expression of Oneness centered around a focused theme. Much like a crystal, my work has many facets to it. I draw my inspiration from ancient and futuristic culture, sacred geometry, divine proportion, progression of the soul, architecture, esoteric symbolism, and nature.

Using my own method of digital imaging, which is rooted in fractal, recursive, or logarithmic mathematics, I begin my work with the time-consuming task of illustrating several different components that will be incorporated into a design. I save each illustration in a graphics library for later reference. Once the components are complete, I begin to weave together and compose all these creations in a mindful way, resulting in one work of art.

Knowing when a design is finished is intuitive. I sense each work is finished when the completed composition begins to speak to my innermost being. My hope for the viewer is that my creations will speak to them in a similar fashion, inspiring them to contemplate and explore the collective consciousness through their own channels of inner wisdom.

At a fundamental level, all my work is a humble attempt to illustrate the multitude of ineffable layers that make up collective consciousness. Emphasis on the void is my primary focus, demonstrated by the black foundation of each piece of art. The void is a creation myth that is talked about in many religious beliefs and cultures from around the world. The images I compose in that black space are symbolic of light, defined as the untapped, unbound, infinite potential that pervades time and space.

Contact Samuel Farrand:

Website: https://www.tetramode.com

Instagram: https://www.instagram.com/samuelfarrand/

Facebook: https://www.facebook.com/samuelfarrand

# REVIEWS

"What stands out to me is how personal Ahriana's book is. This is a compilation not just of theoretical explanations of ritual structures, practices and techniques, but applied ritual as experienced by the many individual contributors who tell their moving accounts of healing and living through sacred rites and rituals. Transformations at the deepest level, profoundly affecting each person's very soul. Grief and celebration; pain and joy; release, rebirth and renewal; recovery and restoration; tears, trauma and triumph; love and laughter; seasons and cycles; connections and correspondences. Sacred ceremony indeed!

This book is a treasure-trove especially for Clergy and others in sacred service, who need to truly understand how rites and rituals can be utilized to deal with life's most challenging and traumatic events."

~ **Oberon Zell,** co-author of
*Creating Circles & Ceremonies: Rites & Rituals For All Seasons & Reasons*

"Rev. Ahriana Platten's book **Rites and Rituals: Harnessing the Power of Sacred Ceremony** is an essential guidebook for healing, purpose, and restoration in times of great chaos. It teaches the importance and power of ritual and ceremony and the how and why.

The power of ritual and ceremony is foundational in my life and the lives of others seeking healing, happiness, and peace. As a healer and spiritual teacher, it is apparent that humanity needs rites, rituals, and ceremonies as much now as at any time on this planet.

Rev. Platten and the featured authors bring many stories of transformation and healing, personally and with groups. Each storyteller illustrates and illuminates the power of ritual, giving guidance and instruction in each chapter.

Though I have experienced and led many ceremonies, I was delighted to find many new and meaningful rituals and rites to add to my toolbox. This is a must read, and an important book for anyone bringing ritual and ceremony to their lives!"

~ **Katherine Skaggs,** Visionary Artist, Teacher, Shamanic Practitioner –
Author of the 2022 COVR Book of the Year, *Artist Shaman Healer Sage:
Timeless Wisdom, Practices, Ritual, and Ceremony
to Transform Your Life and Awaken Your Soul.*

"In the 33 years that I have been a faith leader, I have gone from being a Christian to a Unitarian Universalist to an Ethical Humanist. In all these transformations, ritual has been central to my spiritual practice, both personally and congregationally. In this book, Ahriana Platten has pulled together an amazing collection of rituals that are easily accessible to people from any faith tradition, from experienced ceremonialists to those just dipping their toes into the waters of rites and rituals. Ahriana's thoughtful introduction to rites and rituals, lays a solid foundation based on her years of experience and practice. I will keep this book close at hand for inspiration and am already adapting one of the rituals for use in an upcoming retreat."

~ **Rev. Dr. Nori Rost,** Leader, *New York Society for Ethical Culture*

"As well as offering the gift of Ahriana's own depth of experience and understanding, this book also includes an anthological treasure trove of wisdom from a wide range of practitioners. ***Rites and Rituals'*** powerfully illustrates the value of engaging with mindful intention the rites of passage that punctuate human life. It is an enlightening exploration of the transformative power and healing potential of Sacred Ceremony."

~ **Philip Carr-Gomm**, author of *Druid Mysteries*

"***Rites and Rituals: Harnessing the Power of Sacred Ceremony*** is a masterpiece! It's a map to experiencing one's own embodied wisdom and achieving communion with the Divine. Each ceremony is like a recipe in the cookbook of life. Through inspired storytelling, Ahriana Platten weaves the threads from ancient to modern-day understandings, inviting us in to witness the power and miracles that come from putting feet to our prayers. This book is a gift for any seeker, minister, or leader called to serve love at sacred crossroad moments in time."

~ **Stephanie Urbina Jones,** Bestselling Author of
*Shaman Heart-Turning Pain into Passion and Purpose,*
Co-founder, Freedom Folk and Soul.

"There is perhaps no higher calling than living one's life with purpose and with intention. Recognizing and embracing the power of transitional moments as we grow and change is vital for the actualization of our potential. When sacred times are shared with others, these moments unite us in ways beyond time and space Sacred ceremonies, rites, rituals, and initiations have defined cultures and peoples for thousands of years. Dr. Platten provides an exceptionally riveting performance in introducing or perhaps re-introducing the transforming importance of the sacred ceremony. In today's high-paced lifestyle of constant distraction compounded by a bombardment of stimuli and information, many of us have forgotten the deep magic which exists in important stages of life. All too often we miss pivotal moments or brush past them out of distraction or more often, from pain. In this work, you will find words that touch your very soul, and practices that breathe new life, purpose, and intention from echoes of our ancient past."

~ **Rev. Deacon Bryan Garner,** Order of the Diaconate Apostolic Johannite Church, Author of *Gateways through Stone and Circle,* and *Gateways through Light and Shadow: A True Relation of What Transpired Between Frater Ashen Chassan, His Scryer Benn Mac Stiofán and the Spirits*

"As I read ***Rites and Rituals: Harnessing the Power of Sacred Ceremonies,*** I was struck with a thought, "Finally, someone has crafted information that is not just another how-to-do book about rituals and rites of passage." The words pulled me into what it is to be present when being a conduit to serve communities and individuals in sacred spaces. The authors of the chapters speak with heartfelt stories from their own experiences in ways that teach the need to be awake to others when in service to humanity. The stories are poignant and vulnerable and left me present with differences between rituals, rites of passage, and what ministering at its core is about. I highly recommend ***Rites and Rituals: Harnessing the Power of Sacred Ceremonie*** s to those who want to serve the greater good with open hearts."

~ **Rev. Jerrie K. Hildebrand,** Author, *Pagan and Earth-Centered Voices in Unitarian Universalism* & Minister, Circle Sanctuary

# DISCLAIMER

This book offers spiritual and wellness information, as well as instruction for sacred ceremonial practices, and is designed for educational purposes only. This is an interfaith publication and includes rites and rituals from a variety of spiritual and religious traditions. Each story reflects the personal experience of its author. You should not rely on this information as a substitute for, nor does it replace professional medical advice, diagnosis, or treatment. If you have any concerns or questions about your mental, physical, or emotional health, you should always consult with a physician or other healthcare professional. Do not disregard, avoid, or delay obtaining medical or health related advice from your healthcare professional because of something you may have read here. The use of any information provided in this book is solely at your own risk.

Developments in scientific, spiritual, and medical research may impact the advice that appears here. No assurances can be given that the information contained in this book will always include the most relevant findings or developments with respect to the particular material.

Having said all that, know that the authors here have shared their tools, practices, and knowledge with you with a sincere and generous intent to assist you on your spiritual and wellness journey. Please contact them with any questions you may have about the techniques, ceremonies, or information they provided. They will be happy to assist you further!

# DEDICATION

One day, when I was very little, my mom and I were walking down the
road from our homestead to the mailbox.

"Where is God?" I asked.

"God is in everything," Mom replied.

That simple answer set me on a path
to look for the Holy in everything and everyone.

I dedicate this book to my mom, Joanne Alexander,
and to all the teachers whose bright lights and generous spirits
kept me from stumbling in the dark.

# TABLE OF CONTENTS

# INTRODUCTION

The purpose of this book is to empower you to use rites and rituals to improve your life. Unfortunately, familiar spiritual tools like prayer and limited periods of meditation barely touch the immense pressures we encounter in the 21st century. Dealing with global issues like climate change, political polarization, economic decline, and a brutal pandemic, has left us physically exhausted, mentally traumatized, and incomprehensibly separated from one another.

Since the beginning of time, rites and rituals have been used to expand our spiritual connections and reunite communities. Modern society is obsessed with the future and relentlessly bound by the past. In contrast, rites and rituals bring us into the present – the only place where transformation can genuinely occur. Rites and rituals weave together the frayed edges of the human experience, reconnecting us to each other and the Great Mystery.

The authors who contributed their stories to this collaborative effort reveal their deepest wounds and greatest glories in its pages. Each one found healing and wholeness through rites and rituals. It takes remarkable courage to express such vulnerability. These are real people, like you and me, who offer their intimate life details to help you heal what is broken in mind, body, heart, and soul. I'm honored to bring together such a tender bouquet of wise spirits.

In part one, the first three chapters, I'll share a bit about the spiritual teachings and practices that inform the creation of rites and rituals. Then, in part two – you'll journey through the lives and stories of people who've personally experienced their healing power. Each account includes a rite or ritual you can adapt for yourself.

To get the most benefit from this book, read a chapter, then reflect on what you learned. Take time to journal about your inner considerations and observations and how they relate to your life. This is a book for savoring, not one to be gobbled unconsciously.

Before you begin reading, I invite you to create a sacred space. Light a candle. Sit comfortably in a location where your body is well supported and take a few cleansing breaths. Follow the silver thread that connects you to your ancestors and the ancient teachers whose wisdom initiated this book. Let something more potent than the words move into your being and guide you to the passages that will shift your soul and bring you home to your true heart.

# PART ONE

## THE BASICS OF RITES AND RITUALS

BY REV. AHRIANA PLATTEN, PH.D.

# TRUTH AND SURRENDER

In 11 years, I buried 9 children. Even as a minister, that number is mind-numbing.

Each time a mother or father came to me, shattered into a million pieces, my heart followed suit. I held my composure on the outside, but on the inside, I was screaming in pain -- for them and for myself. I have five children of my own. Mothering a child comes with significant risks, loss being the one no parent dares to imagine.

Not a single death felt acceptable. I listened to the heart-wrenching details each loved one shared, knowing they needed a safe space to tell the whole story. Suicides. Murders. Gruesome motor vehicle accidents. So much tragedy and terror. While I consoled the families to the best of my ability, my own heart was shredded by each event. At home my anxiety and my grief multiplied, and my parenting reflected a deepening fear for the safety of my children.

In Chinese medicine, grief is associated with the lungs. Predictably, cancer struck me there. Within a month of leaving my ministry position, I'd had a part of my left lung removed. "I believe the surgery was a complete success. You're cancer free," the thoracic surgeon said. But I knew I needed to let go of the unprocessed grief I was carrying if I was going to fully heal.

Five months later, I attended a Toltec Sacred Journey Breathwork ritual at a retreat in Teotihuacan, Mexico. I knew I couldn't use the exaggerated breathing techniques that were suggested, but I laid down on a yoga mat under a blanket, closed my eyes, and surrendered myself to the journey.

Maybe it was the power of mass consciousness—I was with twenty-five other people—or perhaps it was my simple exhaustion at carrying the weight of grief. I don't know, exactly. But within about thirty minutes of giving myself over to the possibility of healing, I found myself on my knees, arms extended upward as if I was holding all nine bodies over my head so that the horror I felt at knowing these losses so intimately might be lifted from me.

My heart erupted, and the grief I'd been holding for years poured out of me like lava. I let it flow, unable to hold it in any longer. Finally, after what seemed like a lifetime, my arms lowered, and my hands folded over my chest. I sat back on my heels, noticing the emptiness where grief once lived.

In the darkness, I suddenly sensed the presence of my Hopi teacher. I was stunned because he'd passed away a few years earlier. "Open your heart," he said. My eyes were closed, but I could feel him kneeling in front of me as certainly as he had when he was in the flesh. I don't remember the words, but he prayed using a sacred pipe and penciled a symbol in the air. Then, using a hollow eagle bone, he blew smoke into my heart. I could feel it spiral, starting small, then expanding to fill more and more of the empty space inside. As his prayer traveled inward, what was hurt became whole. Gentle tears of gratitude replaced the pain, and I knew my lungs would heal completely.

Before he left, he gifted me with a white butterfly. A totem. A symbol of freedom and joy. I opened my eyes, stretched into my body, and began to journal.

The ritual was complete—and so was the healing.

CHAPTER 1

# WHAT WISE WOMEN AND MEDICINE MEN KNOW

For as long as humans have walked the earth, rites and rituals have been used to

- heal the mind, body, and spirit
- cleanse and purify
- bless or make holy
- and celebrate

Ancient hunters danced around ceremonial fires in the skins of animals to honor the sacrifice of life and offer thanks for the nourishment given. Plants and herbs were gathered and bundled for burning to keep away illness and ease confusion and pain. Amulets were carved and worn to invoke the power and wisdom of gods and goddesses before important decisions were made. We've always known there's more to life than we can see with our physical eyes—and our ancestral wisdom keepers knew our interconnection was at the core of everything.

Wise women and medicine men still exist. We covenant with Spirit, exchanging prayer for well-being, and turning pain into purpose. Mystics and ministers, priests and priestesses, shamans and elders, live in our modern world, guided by the Holy. We understand the seasons and cycles of life, the liminal space in which transformation occurs, and we know how to access the collaborative energies of the natural world. We incorporate the teachings of ancient traditions, quantum science, and neuro-spirituality to bring about unexpected and sometimes unexplainable change.

Over the past forty years, I've traveled the world and led hundreds of rites and rituals. I've shared ceremonies with indigenous elders from 250 tribes and traditions at a global gathering in India, meditated with monks in a Buddhist temple thousands of years old in South Korea, and chanted with nuns in an ancient cathedral in Hungary. I've guided people through initiatory ceremonies from dusk to dawn around sacred fires in the U.S. and served as an Ambassador for the Parliament of The World's Religions, offering ceremonies for people of many faiths. I've coordinated vigils and protective circles where violence occurred, and I spent eleven years as the lead minister for a spiritual community where I live. There, I used rites and rituals daily to help hundreds of people move through every kind of life situation.

Whether passing on sacred stories around a bonfire, praying bedside with a grieving family at the end of life, guiding an initiate across the first gate of empowerment, or humbly washing the feet of the people I served, rites and rituals provided a passage to transformation and healing -- so, when I say rites and rituals work, I'm speaking from a rich history of experience.

Rites, rituals, and sacred ceremonies provide gateways and portals of power when there seems to be no path forward. What might otherwise take years happens in moments. It's both simple and complex.

## RITES AND RITUALS HELP US

- overcome limiting beliefs
- identify and change self-sabotaging behaviors
- heal emotional wounds from traumatic experiences
- discover and embrace inner power
- bring deeper meaning and significance to daily life

Before we explore the stories of those who've been transformed by rites and rituals, let me share some of the teachings and tools that have been shared with me over the years by the teachers, spiritual guides, and wisdom keepers who taught me. These tools and teachings form the foundation of my work in the world. They're not written in any particular order because learning spiritual practices is not linear. It's more of a circular process that invites you to unlearn what you've been taught in order to reveal who you really are.

CHAPTER 2

# POWER, INTENTION, AND EDUCATION

Rites and rituals are processes and formulas that provide uncommon yet effective methods for creating and moving through change. For example, a simple talking stick ritual improves communication between two people or a whole community. A talking stick is an instrument of democracy used by many tribes. I use it for community gatherings and also in pastoral counseling for couples.

"This is a talking stick," I explain, as I hand a natural wooden rod with unique carvings and colorful feathers to someone in the circle. "It's a tribal tool. Whoever has the talking stick has the floor, and we don't interrupt them. If you don't have the talking stick, your job is to listen."

People respect the talking stick because an experience is more meaningful when we connect to history and tradition. Its beauty and power are ritualized by its regular use. "I can't believe how much it helped us to hear each other," one of my clients recently expressed. "We'll make one with our kids and teach them to use it."

A talking stick is a straightforward ritual technique that anyone can apply. It's a great example of a simple way a ritual tool can be used to navigate a specific type of situation. You can use any branch or stick as a talking stick. It doesn't have to be fancy – but I find that decorating it makes people take it more seriously.

Rites and rituals open hearts and clear minds. They help us to embody reverence and allow us to get in touch with our emotions and desires. They provide safe ways to make a change.

## THE DIFFERENCE BETWEEN A RITE AND A RITUAL

*'Rite'* and *'ritual'* are not just different words for the same thing.

*Rites of passage mark life events.* Getting your driver's license or turning twenty-one and legally entering a bar are examples of the secular rites of passage most of us experience.

In the spiritual world, a rite of passage is usually created for a person crossing into a new stage of life. For example, rites of passage are held for people getting married or divorced or for those becoming parents. A rite of passage can honor an advancement in education or punctuate the end of life. *Rites of passage don't happen every day and are often done differently for different people.* They're processes for moving from one state of being to another; single person to married person, parent to grandparent, candidate to president.

*On the other hand, rituals can happen daily and are usually done in nearly the same way each time.* Less process and more practice, rituals deepen our life experiences each time we do them. For example, I have a ritual of making my bed every day. I wasn't always committed to getting my bed made. Something happened that changed the way I look at bed-making. Indulge me in this short explanation:

About 25 years ago, I was at a Native American Church ceremony. It was a beautiful gathering under the stars, and we prayed together until well past midnight. Bobby, a young man in attendance, was unable to take the bus to his next destination because the buses had stopped running hours earlier.

"You can stay at my house if you need a place," I told Bobby.

"Thank you," he said. "I'll take the bus in the morning."

When we got home, Bobby laid his bedroll on the living room floor. He seemed careful to smooth out every wrinkle and lay things out in a specific way, but I didn't give that much thought. The next morning, I woke up earlier than usual and headed to the kitchen for coffee. I noticed that Bobby was up already and had neatly folded his bedding, tying it together with a colorful rope. "Can you teach my kids to make their beds when they get up?" I asked jokingly.

"One of my elders taught me that your bed is the altar upon which you place your body when you go into the dream time," Bobby explained.

"That's why I always make my bed right away when I get up. It keeps the space sacred."

The ritual of making the bed is something I've done daily since Bobby shared that teaching with me. It's more than a habit. It's a ritual that focuses my energy on the dreamtime. Doing it in the morning changes everything about how I feel when it's time to fold back the covers and get in my bed at night. I say a silent prayer of thanks when I get up, then neatly make my bed so that the altar where my body rests while I dream is always lovingly cared for. Then, when I go to bed, it feels like a safe and holy place.

Brushing your teeth can become a ritual if you partner it with an intention of some kind, like this affirmation:

*"As I brush my teeth, I prepare my mouth for speaking healing words today."*

Journaling each day can be a ritual when partnered with a prayer to open your heart more deeply each time you record your experiences. *Rituals are repeated practices that evoke personal growth or spiritual expansion in a duplicatable fashion.*

We often use the word ceremony interchangeably with the words rite and ritual. "Ceremony" can describe the processes and practices we use to move through rites and rituals, *or "ceremony" can be used to replace either "rite" or "ritual" when describing a process or practice.* Sacred ceremonies are spiritually-based rites and rituals created to facilitate transformation.

## ATTENTION AND INTENTION

To learn, grow, or change, we must *pay* attention. It's the *cost* of transformation. We *pay attention* to what our senses tell us. We *pay attention* to the details of our spiritual practices. We *pay attention* to the guidance that comes from a variety of sources.

But attention alone is not enough. When it comes to rites and rituals, *attention* must be partnered with *intention*. What do you *intend* to transform? How would you describe the outcome you wish to create? Asking yourself these questions will help you be precise when constructing a rite or ritual.

In the case of a wedding, we want to shift the way two individuals relate to one another. The outcome we're looking for is an unbreakable union of hearts. In the case of ritualized healing, our desire is to move someone from a state of dis-ease of mind, body, or spirit into a state of ease and wellness in which the wounded aspect of self is measurably improved.

The *intention* of any rite or ritual must be defined early on. A map is useless without a destination in mind. Therefore, one of the first steps in mapping out a rite or ritual is to clarify the desired outcome.

*Pay attention to your intention.* Be very specific. The more clarity you have, the more likely it is that your rite or ritual will work.

Be careful, especially with words. Here's a quick example of how poorly chosen words can result in a less-than-satisfying outcome. For several years, I produced an upscale event for women. Then, one year, I decided to reserve the most beautiful ballroom in the city. It was majestic, with gold inlaid soffits, rich brocade wallpaper, and massive crystal chandeliers. I could see the whole thing in my head—every woman arriving in her finest evening wear, a string quartet filling their ears with elegant music, and a dinner feast so delicious it hushed the room. I did a little ceremony to help assure the energies lined up for what I wanted, and inadvertently I mumbled an almost inaudible intention, "I just have to make enough money to pay for it."

I didn't consider the statement an intention – but over the next few weeks, I said it repeatedly. That sentence became a worry-filled mantra. "I just have to make enough money to pay for it."

Everything happened exactly as I imagined. The women were stunning, the music serene, and the food even tastier than expected -- and I made just enough money, *to the penny,* to pay for the event – and not one dime more.

I got exactly what I created with my words -- and my worry.

"Be careful what you ask for – you might get it." It's one of the first things I was told by a spiritual teacher. Trust me. It's an easy lesson to forget. Pay attention to your intention.

## IT'S NOT ABOUT "WOO-WOO" – ITS ABOUT ENERGY AND COSMIC LAW

The Sanskrit or Vedic religious concept of *rtá* – or cosmic law, the reliable operating principle of the universe – is one way to understand how rites and rituals work. The word itself has etymological ties to related words like harmony, art, and the word 'ritual.' The term *rtá* suggests we live in a finely tuned universe, and that adherence to cosmic law provides us with creative power we can use for transformation.

In the 21st century, science and spirituality are dovetailing, and the ancient mysteries we previously considered supernatural or illusionary are being explained by modern-day research. Science is helping us understand cosmic law. If the Big Bang theory is correct, it confirms that all life is interconnected, made of the same star stuff, began in the same place, and is inter-reliant. Wisdom keepers have been telling us that all life is interconnected and inter-reliant for as long as words have been spoken. Interconnection and inter-reliance are fundamental to the way rites and rituals work.

Appropriate use of energy is also fundamental. We're understanding more about energy through scientific research on topics like quantum entanglement, string theory, and the study of collective consciousness. Science is proving what wisdom keepers and medicine people always knew -- when we tap into the power of universal energy and interconnection, we can improve ourselves and our world. Rites and rituals provide ways to tap into both.

## KEEP IT SIMPLE, SWEETHEART

Over the past forty years, I've experimented with simple rites and rituals and with very complex spiritual practices. "Simple" is so much more powerful than one might imagine. Once upon a time, I used a very simple spiritual process to help ease the fear of an entire community. Imagine you're with me, in the lobby of the spiritual center, early on a Sunday morning. Here's the story:

"The whole neighborhood's burning. I don't even know if I still have a home."

She was one of many that entered that day. Some were stone-faced and emotionless, frozen like winter's first snow turns the green earth hard and cold. Some showed signs of exhaustion after sleepless nights in a shelter or on a friend's couch. Wordless stares replaced our usual happy buzz, and smoke hung thick outside the doors. A few miles away, a roaring blaze, hundreds of feet high, consumed the mountainside.

A billowing plume of smoke is never a good sign when you live in the Rockies. I saw it first on the summer solstice. Within 48 hours, people were evacuated from their homes, and within a week, a fiery dragon of destruction descended into the city, swallowing structures whole.

I was shocked by my body's instinctual reaction to the smell of smoke and the embers floating in the air. Even in the daylight, they glowed, advancing miles into the city on a blustery wind that fanned the flames and grew the beast. At one point, the entire mountain range to the west seemed to be on fire. The haze made my eyes sting. *I've got to get out of here! Fire moves fast. These hundred-year-old houses are nothing but kindling to a blaze like that!* The voice in my head relentlessly begged me to find safety. Thankfully, my concern for the community was stronger than my fear.

Standing in the lobby of the spiritual center as people entered, my mind was buzzing. *What's the right thing to say when people are scared? This would be a terrible time to say the wrong thing! Do I ask if they've been evacuated? Maybe not. Maybe just wait and see what they say. But will they think I don't care if I don't ask?* These concerns left me feeling unsettled and uncertain -- not a good state to be in when you're expected to deliver a calming spiritual message that helps others to feel strong in the face of a crisis.

As I welcomed them into sacred space, I was met with hollow, empty eyes. We greeted each other with that numb kind of expression you have when something is incredibly wrong. The world was gray, and so were the faces. "Have *you* been evacuated?" they whispered. A few asked if I needed anything. Most were silent or simply offered a shallow "Good morning" as they entered.

*Come on, Spirit! What am I gonna say? If there was ever a time I needed your help, it's now!*

Suddenly, as if the sky opened to deliver it, an idea fell into my head, and I knew exactly what to do.

"Go get me the biggest clay bowl we have," I said to Crystal, a friend who always seems to be in the right place at the right time.

"Do you need a table?" she asked, reading my mind.

"Yeah—the tall one with the plant on it. Put the plant on my desk."

In moments, she returned with a huge piece of blue pottery safely tucked under one arm and a four-foot-high plant stand in her other hand. She gave them both to me.

"Water?"

"Yes—two pitchers."

"On it." She was back in a flash.

I prayed as I poured the water, watching it wrap its way around the soft curves of the vessel. Finally, it settled like a reflection pool just below the lip of the bowl. People found their seats and watched as I leaned in to give the music director a few last-minute instructions.

"Play the opening song, then I'll say a few words, and when I start the ceremony, just noodle around a bit on the Clavinova until we're done."

Connie's a pro. She didn't need any more direction than that. We opened the service, and while she sang the opening song, I contemplated the fearful eyes of our community. I took a deep breath, knowing that, somehow, the right words would come when I opened my mouth.

"Good morning," I said with borrowed confidence. "I know you're scared. We're all scared. That just means our bodies are working to protect us. The fear we're feeling is instinct doing its job, and that's a good thing. But I want you to consider that, at the moment, we're safe. And even though it doesn't seem like it with all the smoke, we're several miles from the fire. So, what should we do with our time together this morning?

They just stared at me.

"Let's release our fear," I said matter-of-factly.

"Remember how we line up to light our candles on Christmas Eve? Let's do that. Just line up in the aisles and come forward when I motion for you. Then, when it's your turn, place your fingertips in this bowl and release the fire." (Yes, I said "fire instead of "fear"—because water quenches fire. Words matter at times like this.)

"Don't overthink it. Just do it. Release the fire into the water."

They lined up, seemingly relieved to have someone give them direction.

After speaking a blessing out loud to thank the water for accepting what we were about to release, I motioned the first person forward. The familiarity of the music was already softening them as, one by one, they dipped their fingers in the cool puddle of healing liquid.

Big, tall, muscular men. Mothers with little children who needed to be lifted up to reach the bowl. Silver-haired seniors. Each took a turn. They placed their fingers in the water. Almost immediately, spontaneous tears began to flow. It happened repeatedly, like a contagion passing from one person to the next. Frozen emotions melted in the warm elixir, giving way to a stream of release. Tears ran down my face as I connected with each heart that stood before the bowl.

In this simple and profoundly emotional way, our fear was dissolved and replaced with a powerful sense of community connection. People who were cold, numb, and empty-eyed became warm, centered, and alive. The color returned to their faces, and their posture changed from stiff and guarded to soft and at ease.

A simple bowl of water, a table, and an intention. That's all that was needed.

Oh yeah—and the courage to trust the spiritual guidance I received.

## "CAPITAL-L" LOVE

As I mentioned, rites and rituals are often called "ceremonies." The title of this book specifies *sacred* ceremonies to create an understanding that Spirit is primary to what's being offered here. The word *sacred* can be defined as something connected with God, Goddess, deities of any kind, or dedicated to a spiritual purpose. It's advantageous to connect with what feels holy to you. *The Indwelling God, the Great Mystery, the Creator, the One-of-a-Thousand-Names-and-Faces, Quantum Consciousness, Universal Mind.*

Why is this important? Because the presence of the Holy opens the door to transformation for everyone involved. My personal experience is that when I involve the *"more-than-me"* that lives through me, as me, and all around me, my rites and rituals work better. I never do ceremonies alone. I invite the Holy and pay attention to the guidance that comes in unique and empowering ways.

You can refer to the Holy by whatever name you choose. I can assure you the power is not in the name. Universal Love - by whatever name you choose - is the underlying power needed for all rites, rituals, and sacred ceremonies. I often refer to it as Capital "L" Love. It's what we're all made of and what connects us to each other. It's where my guidance comes from and the substance of all sacred work.

# STANDING AT THE THRESHOLD

I was 17 when I was awakened to the power of ceremony on a beach in Salvador, Bahia, Brazil. Being an exchange student in 1978 provided a unique kind of freedom. There was no social media. Long-distance calls were incredibly expensive and rarely made, and I was completely free to be myself in a way I'd never been in my life – thousands of miles from the watchful eyes of my parents.

One night, I was traveling with a pack of locals, headed out for a night of reggae music and dancing, when we happened upon a beachfront gathering of women, mid-ritual in the tradition of the Afro-Brazilian Candomblé religion.

Across the sandy beach, I could see a bonfire burning. Synchronized drums pounded out a sacred rhythm. Silhouettes of dancing bodies circled the flame, moving and swaying in time with the music. The closer I got, the more captivated I was. In the rhythm of the chant, I could make out one word—"Lemanja."

*What does it mean?*

There was no Google to look it up, just the rolling waves, the sultry summer breeze, and an intense warmth rising in my chest. Their heads were wrapped in white lace and covered by beaded seashell crowns. They were dressed in layered skirts of white and turquoise, and the intensity of the energy they were raising pulled me in like a siren singing a sailor toward imagined ecstasy.

"Come on. The disco is this way," my Brazilian friend hollered. But I couldn't move. I was trance-fixed, in the truest sense of the word. Nothing mattered but my heartbeat, the way it pulsed with their song, and my longing for connection to. . .*what? What was calling me?*

"Wait. What does it mean—Lemanja?"

"Goddess of the sea," my host said, visibly annoyed that I wasn't moving toward what waited at the local nightclub.

"I can't go with you."

Spirit stopped me in my tracks. I couldn't walk away. I don't know how long I stood there watching, inching closer and closer, but more than forty years later, I still don't have words to explain what was changed in me that evening. My soul was awakened and inspired. Even now, the experience is as potent and alive in my memory as it was the day it happened. I long to return to the dance, the flame, and the rhythm of my heart. I ache for the deep connection to a Goddess I'd never heard of but in whose presence I felt whole, alive, and connected to everything and everyone.

That experience launched my journey to understand the energy of sacred ceremony and brought me to sit at the feet of many masters. At 17, I had much to learn.

## WHAT GIVES US THE AUTHORITY TO DO RITES AND RITUALS?

The short answer is that your authority comes from the same source as your very breath.

*Life. God. Source. Great Mystery. The Universe.*

As a living, breathing human, you have every right to make your life experience more sacred. No intercessor is necessary. You can pray, light candles, meditate, chant, and use many other methods to connect with the God-of-your-knowing.

When I was about 11, a priest chastised me for wanting to be an altar girl. At that time, there was no such thing. Females were not allowed to serve in that way. He lectured me about the fall of Eve and said, "you are never to step up on the altar unless you're here to clean, I call you up for something, or you're getting married." For a moment, I felt the pain of the God I'd grown to love rejecting me – but after more consideration, I realized it wasn't God. It was a person. Someone just like me, only a little older. I resolved to take charge of my spiritual experience, claiming a level of sovereignty that led me to cultivate a strong personal relationship with the Great Mystery.

No other person has more access to the Divine than you do. The only difference is that some people have studied more than you and have more tools and techniques at their fingertips. That's why finding a good spiritual teacher is so beneficial. I've been deeply blessed to work with master teachers from spiritual traditions around the world, and even today, I continue to pursue new knowledge and experience. The reason is simple – I want to go deeper. The more I learn, the more thoroughly immersed in my spiritual experience I can be.

If you want to perform ceremonies for others or deepen your own ceremonial experiences, the best advice I can give you is to find a master teacher. There are several amongst the contributing authors in part two of this book. Check out their bios at the end of each chapter to find someone who interests you, or feel free to reach out to me for assistance.

A word of caution: Over the years, I've come to understand that not everyone should engage in performing ceremonies for other people. There's a code of ethics, both inherent and learned, that you must be willing to live by if you wish to be a ceremonialist. This includes respect for free will and a steadfast commitment to service. *If you plan to offer rites and rituals for others, please consider getting some training before you start.* It will help you to understand the ethical implications, put down your ego, ask the right questions of those you serve, and expand your base of tools and techniques.

Remember this—Rites, rituals, and ceremonies change lives. If you choose to step into a calling as a ceremonialist, it comes with the weight of responsibility for your actions. Learn how to do ceremonies well and ethically.

For now—if you're ready to create rites and rituals for yourself, keep reading!

# CHAPTER 3

# SEASONS AND CYCLES

*Fascinating. These people are willing to stand in the brutal Texas sun just to get his blessing.*

Elksinger was a bigger-than-life character whose reputation as a metaphysician preceded him. I couldn't tell his age, but he was old in comparison to my 31 years. He was an iconic mixture of gray hair, flowing robes, and sweeping gestures. "Merlinesque," I'd say when describing him later in the day. It was evident by his demeanor that he wielded ancient wisdom.

Glistening beads of perspiration gathered on my brow as I waited in line. We were quiet in that reverent way one is quiet when entering a cathedral. I observed how he spoke to each person, challenging them, clearing them of unseen energies, and anointing them with an oil of eucalyptus, cinnamon, and clove. It felt like fire when he touched my forehead. Have you ever seen those weighted blow-up clowns that little children play with? You punch them, and they rock to the ground, then immediately bounce back up. That's what I experienced inside my body. Elksinger drew a symbol on my forehead with the oil and used his breath to charge it. When he did, my kinesthetic body bounced out of me and immediately bounced right back into my physical form. My mind started spinning.

*What just happened?! Oh my God. This is real!* Standing there, I tried to rationalize something that simply wasn't rational. Elksinger wrapped me in a warm, welcoming hug, stepped back, looked into my eyes with a knowing gaze, and said, "Welcome to this sacred space." He placed his hand on my back to steady me and guided me into the circle. I crossed the threshold.

Thresholds are exciting places. They move us from one state of being to the next. We cross a threshold to go outside and come back in. When designing a sacred ceremony, we create a threshold that moves us from where we are to where we want to be.

*A spiritual threshold is frequently referred to as liminal space,* a boundary or transitional point between two conditions or ways of life. Whether you're moving from dis-ease to well-being, childhood to adolescence, or novice to initiate, metamorphosis begins at a threshold.

Creating a well-defined threshold is one of the keys to achieving the outcome you desire from your rite or ritual.

Thresholds are both physical and spiritual. For example, in the physical world, we might decorate a doorway, create an altar, and wear specific garments or jewelry to help designate a place and time of change. Likewise, anything we can see, sense, taste, hear, or feel will assist us in stepping into a liminal space.

A threshold is a combination of prayer, intention, and sovereign assignment. You designate the place for transformation, invoke Spiritual Presence to support you, and begin your work there.

## INVOCATION AND EVOCATION

As has been said, the intention is everything when it comes to spiritual work. And invocation is one process for enacting our intention to create liminal space.

What does it mean to *invoke?*

Simply put, you're calling in or inviting Spiritual Presence.

You might call that Presence by a name. For example, "I call to you, Diana, empowering Goddess of Women, to bless this sacred site and offer your strength to those in this circle." Or "I call this ceremony to the attention of Jesus the Christ, beloved son of the father. Bless those who cross this threshold with the change their hearts desire."

If you're uncomfortable with archetypes, you might create your threshold with an affirmation. For example, "I create a threshold through my words and intentions. This is a place of transformation."

"Say it's so, and it is," Elksinger once told me.

For the work ahead, you should also be familiar with *evocation.* To *evoke* is to call something from inside yourself to the surface of your being. For example, you might evoke a state of being like strength or gentleness, or you could evoke your higher self. Your rite or ritual will evoke change within you and call it forward.

## LOCATIONS FOR SACRED CEREMONY

I've held ceremonies at the top of a ski run, in a ghost town, under a flowering tree in a botanic garden, in my living room, in an ancient temple, in an aspen grove, in a red tent, at a crossroads (watch for traffic), in a cemetery, and on a boat dock before a group of us went white water rafting. Rites and rituals can be held in any number of places. Whether inside or outside, on top of a building, or under a Chuppah, your location has significance and impacts your experience.

What feeling do you want to inspire in those who attend? I love outdoor ceremonies. Something about the breeze kissing my cheek feels holy to me. However, when privacy is needed, like when I'm doing healing work for someone who's experienced trauma, I usually choose an indoor space that's safe, comfortable, and offers little chance for disturbance.

One of my teachers was known to say, "If you can't do it in the parking lot of Safeway, you can't do it all." I agree with that.

Ceremonies sometimes need to happen wherever you are. If you witness a car accident, you'll probably pray and send energy to the people involved. Is that a sacred ceremony? Absolutely. Prayer and intention put you in liminal space-- the space between *before people were hurt* and *when the hurt has been addressed.* Prayer at this threshold can be potent because your emotions are intense, and your mind automatically focuses on the well-being of those involved. When the body, mind, and emotions are united in effort, Spirit collaborates with us, giving power to our intentions.

Be thoughtful about the location you choose for your rites and rituals. Your location can amplify or reduce the strength of your transformative work.

## THE SEASONS AND CYCLES OF SACRED CEREMONY

"To everything, there is a season," scripture says. *I wonder if he thought about the seasons when he was writing?*

My beloved's arm rested on the back of my chair as we settled in to listen to a lecture by Richard Louv, author of *Last Child in The Woods.* Hanging on every word, I found myself unintentionally nodding as he spoke because what he was saying lined up so perfectly with what I knew to be true.

"Some believe we have dominion over the earth. Others believe we're stewards of the earth. The truth is, we *are* the earth." These words put into context something I've always known; we're no more and no less important than every other creature or being on the planet and in the universe. We're not only interconnected, but we're also inter-reliant, and what we do affects everyone and everything.

Each day, you can walk outside and breathe oxygen supplied by the trees and plants around you. The temperature tickling your skin tells you how to dress. The presence of the sun or the moon informs your actions. The flutter of wings overhead or a rustle in the underbrush reminds you that you're seen and heard as you move about. At times, the natural world feels welcoming. At other times, it pushes you away because its power feels dangerous and mighty. I often feel both these sensations at the ocean's edge. Its size and power overwhelm me, yet I'm drawn into the caress of its rolling waves as they meet the shore.

What would it be like if we lived consciously as part of the earth rather than walking on it like a parasite with little regard for its host? Experience tells me that when we realize we *are* the earth, we make better choices for ourselves and all living things.

Ancient people on all continents shared an intimate connection to the earth and its seasons and cycles. Without knowledge of the energy of each season, the people would perish. They followed the stars, planted by the phases of the moon, and took only what they needed, leaving enough for others. Sadly, we've lost connection to nature. Few of us can find our way without a GPS, could name what the next phase of the moon will be, or even understand the significance of each phase. The knowledge still exists, but we've stopped *paying attention,* and consequently, we've become disconnected from the very source of our day-to-day existence.

What has this to do with rites and rituals? It's a matter of timing. While we can perform rites and rituals at any time, when we follow the natural energy of the earth we're inseparably connected to, the energy of our ceremonies will be stronger and more effective.

Let's look at the seasons and cycles of life.

# WINTER, SPRING, SUMMER, FALL—
# TIMING MATTERS

We all have a favorite season. During winter, people enjoy fires and snuggling up with a good book, while in summer, people love bike riding and eating sweet peaches ripened in the warm sun. These are generalizations, of course, but you get the picture. Why do we prefer one season over the other? It has to do with comfort, lifestyle, memories from our childhood, and so much more. The bottom line is this; every season offers something unique. When it comes to rites and rituals, every season provides the perfect energy and environment for a particular type of experience.

Traditionally, we think of spring as the beginning of the cycle of seasons, but I'll begin with winter and explain as we go.

## WINTER

Have you ever noticed how quiet the earth is when it rests under a soft blanket of fresh snow? It's as peaceful as the gentle breathing of a mother watching her newborn sleep. I often feel afraid to make a sound that might interrupt the beauty of the moment. Winter is the season of rest. Falling between autumn's dying off and spring's awakening, winter gives us pause from the outside world. It's a time when growth is slow, and much of life is in a state of hibernation. The deep chill suggests we find a blanket, cozy up, and sip honey-laden tea. We know that, soon enough, spring will come, and with it, new possibilities for life. We needn't think so much about creation in the dark of winter. Instead, winter is an introspective time that invites us to slow down, be still, journey within, and contemplate life's deeper meanings. To generate the energy needed to begin something new, we require downtime. Rest precedes birth. Every mother knows that a baby will become still in the womb for a period before its arrival. The wisdom of the womb tells the child to stop kicking and save energy for the journey of emergence. In like fashion, we rest in the cave-like womb of winter before the power of spring calls us into our next creative cycle.

Because winter energy is not creative energy, I recommend against making New Year's resolutions. They interrupt our much-needed rest. While the turning of each year invites us to consider what we want to change, New Year's resolutions rarely manifest.

Winter is the perfect time for rites and rituals that honor the wisdom of age. It's a good time for journaling, contemplative practices, and self-care rituals. Dreaming can be powerful when ritualized in winter.

## SPRING

Imagine a seed as winter's melting snow softens the cold, hard ground. Every droplet of water that seeps into the soil finds its way to the shell that holds life within, coaxing it to crack and give way. And when it does, life, so small and tender, must push its way out and seek the sun's warmth. *Which way is up?*

I sometimes feel like I don't know my way when spring begins. If I fail to rest enough in winter, I feel a bit groggy and unclear in early spring. As a result, it's harder to manifest momentum for the creative process in my life – but the energy of awakening comes fairly quickly.

When spring arrives, the earth beneath our feet is alive. It's as though the whole planet is waking up with dreams to share. Spring is a time for seeds, quickening, and birth. It's a time of immaculate conception.

Not unique to a single faith, immaculate conception stories appear in both ancient and modern religious traditions. Immaculate conception is the story of a birth that results from intercourse with the Divine. Outside the laws of human life, which require sperm and egg, spiritual conception happens to all of us.

Immaculate conception stories are spread across many religions and traditions because they teach us about our relationship with the Divine Mind . Have you ever had an idea that seemed to pop up out of nowhere? I'm not talking about the outcome of analytical consideration. I'm talking about an idea you didn't expect. Maybe it came in a dream or dropped wholly into your mind. Where do you think that idea came from? If you didn't think it up, who did? Union with the Holy happens like that. In the dream time, the Holy inspires. When our minds wander, the Holy shines a light on the untraveled path. And sometimes, the Holy comes barging in with a new idea in broad daylight with no warning. We're inspired through intimate connection with the Holy and conceive ideas that awaken us to our potential, especially in early spring.

Once a new idea is conceived, it quickens in the belly of our consciousness, kicking and wiggling inside in the undeniable way a growing child kicks in the womb. Eventually, we birth something beautiful through our actions and creative endeavors.

Spring is an excellent time for new beginnings. It's the time for initiatory rites, for blessing the seeds you'll plant in your real or proverbial garden, and for ceremonies committing yourself to a new creative endeavor.

## SUMMER

So why do marriages traditionally happen in June if spring is the time of new beginnings? Because, in summer, life matures, and maturity is essential to sacred unions like marriage.

In the summertime, what was born in the spring is pulled into greater being by the sun's energy. Pay attention to the summer solstice. It can be an intense time. At the sun's zenith, life sizzles with activity. We're energized and called into action. It's time for growth. In the summer sun, plants grow tall so fast we can almost watch them gain their height. New leaves sprout every day, and budding flowers bloom, sending a signal to bees and other pollinators that the season of work has arrived.

In early summer, we're under Sol's most substantial influence. We pull weeds from our garden and pluck out the distractions that get in the way of our future harvest. The long days and warm nights provide extended time to weed, grow, and flourish. Early summer is a powerful season of fire, which makes it a good time to burn what has served its purpose. Destruction can be healthy and wise. Release old journals full of pain, letters from past lovers who've moved on, prayers, and processes that are complete or will never be completed. I like to burn old legal documents and release the energy from conflict in the early summer.

And lest we exhaust ourselves completely through our efforts, summer provides a brief reprieve in the season of ripening. By the middle of this season, the fruit is on the vine. It hangs there, basking in the warmth of the sun until its skin grows bright with color and its insides are soft and juicy. What makes your skin grow colorful and your life feel juicy and sweet? Vacation! Midsummer is a wonderful time to camp, travel, connect with friends, and enjoy the sweetness of life. The first harvest is just around the corner, so time to soak up the sun is precious. Ceremonies related to coming into your personal power are well placed here. It's also a good time to visit a sacred site for the first time and bask in its energy.

## FALL

And, before you know it, fall arrives, and with it, the nourishment of the harvest. It's fun to gather the fruits of our labor. But, its also work to gather those fruits. By autumn, we're reaping what we've sown. Whether it's zucchini or experience, this is the time to take an accounting of what we've been growing. It's time to call our friends together to share our bounty. Gardeners know too much zucchini will rot on the vine. You give some away because you can't possibly eat everything you've grown. The same is true with knowledge and accomplishment. Autumn is the season to share what you've gained, to give something away that will help another, and to support the community that supports you.

It's a time of release. Just like leaves fall from a tree, escaping the bondage of the branches, autumn is the time for you to release old ideas and ways of being that keep you captive. The journey of a leaf doesn't end in its escape. Leaves dance on the wind, swirling and spinning, greeting the ground tenderly. They entertain us by crunching beneath our feet. In time, they'll break down and make the soil more fertile. Similarly, things we release find new value. They nourish what will be grown in the future.

In autumn, we honor our partnership with death and its walk beside us every step of our lives. Adolescence dies to make way for adulthood. One job passes, and the next appears. Relationships die, and we gain wisdom from the endings that will lead us to a better kind of relationship in the future. People die and move on to whatever comes after this world. Beliefs die to make way for new types of consciousness.

Death is a blessed companion that helps us evolve.

Autumn is the season for reflecting on what has been and for honoring the death of people and things. As we move toward the darkness, we reflect on our experiences, release what no longer serves us, and honor death as a balancing and critical aspect of life. In autumn, we set up altars to honor our ancestors, release what no longer serves us, and prepare for the season of rest that will come with winter.

In today's world, most of us move through this spiraling cycle blindly rather than with the kind of great attention and interest our ancestors had. If we can regain our awareness of seasons and cycles, we can dramatically change our lives and the lives of the people around us.

# EARTH, AIR, FIRE, WATER– ELEMENTAL INFLUENCES

"You learn about the elements by walking with them," my teacher told me. "Go find the wind."

I did as she asked, heading to the top of a hill where there was usually a gentle breeze. It was a bit of a hike, and on the way up, I began wondering what I'd do if there was no wind when I arrived. Almost as quickly as the thought passed through my mind, I felt my hair lift away from my head, caught in a gusty gale.

"Tell me what you want from me."

Its voice was breathy and wild.

*I want to know you.*

In the silence of my mind, I entered a conversation with the invisible force.

"Then you must become me," said the wind.

I sat down on the ground, releasing my imagination to do its work. Soon I was enveloped in a giddy sense of freedom and flow, rising and falling, swirling and turning—unpredictable and full of joy.

I've been talking with nature for as long as I can remember. Trees, birds, stones, rivers, and clouds all have something to say if you take the time to listen. Sometimes they speak in words, but more often, they communicate in images and feelings. All creation emerges from the living energy of the Holy, a power that gives life to all things.

Four elements correspond with the seasons and directions. Different spiritual traditions move these elements around. For our purpose, I'll share them as they've been taught to me.

- Earth corresponds to winter and the north.
- Air corresponds to spring and the east.
- Fire corresponds to summer and the south.
- Water corresponds to autumn and the west.

These four are more than the physical aspects you've come to know. If you understand elemental influences, you'll easily find meaningful words and stirring symbols to use at the threshold of your ceremonies. Begin by going to meet them. Look for the wind. Let it caress your skin. Place your feet in the water and allow its energy to wash through you. Warm your hands at the fire and dance with its flickering flames. Lay your body on the earth and feel the strong reliability of its embrace. The elements are living energies. Let me share a bit about them:

## EARTH

Earth is the ground we walk on, our foundation. On mountaintops, in silent caves, on sandy shores, and along city sidewalks, the earth rests below our feet. Like us, its moving energy teems with potential. Its qualities are like a stone; strong, steadfast, sometimes rocky and jagged, other times smooth and cool. When we speak in our rites and rituals, we can refer to these qualities as metaphors for what we hope to change. For example, when a spiritual teacher commits to a student, he or she might say, "As the earth is solid and holds us with unquestionable stability, I give you my commitment to hold your heart and share these sacred teachings." I like to use crystals and stones on my altar to remind me of the qualities of the earth and the strength of its wisdom.

## AIR

Air surrounds us, fills our lungs with life-giving oxygen, whips our hair around, and tears at our clothing when it's blustery. It heralds qualities in life that move us like the clouds are driven by a breeze. Without air to fill our lungs, we can't speak. With it, we speak words that shape our world, sing songs that heal our hearts, whisper prayers and blessings, and breathe hope into our creations.

Here's a simple air blessing you could use in any ceremony: "May you be blessed by the breath of the invisible that inspires you and sings joy into your heart."

I use many symbols for air. Bells, feathers, and music bring the element to life. Incense and essential oils are great tools for bringing the olfactory sense into your rite or ritual.

## FIRE

You'll find it in passionate encounters, willful conflicts, a warm embrace, and an energetic and enthusiastic speech. Fire can be so hot it burns through things and so soothing that it gently warms a room and brings comfort where there's pain. It both blazes and flickers, feeds, and consumes. Here's an example of how we might bless a home using fiery words:

"May your new home be filled with a light so luminous that it opens your eyes to every blessing within its walls. May you find warmth and comfort here."

Candles are prominent symbols of fire. I love to build an actual fire when there's a place for it. Fire is terrific for burning what needs to be released and invoking insights.

## WATER

Oceans, rivers, streams. Floods and flowing fountains. The fluid of birth and a cleansing agent for life. We're mostly made of water; like it, we ebb and flow—in love, anger, joy, and sadness. Water is the seat of emotion. Tears break down walls between people and open us to our wildest nature. In rites and rituals, water is used to bless, purify, cleanse, and blend energies. Water flows where it wants to go. It avoids obstacles and creates its own path. It converges and becomes more powerful in its collaborations. If we want a soul to travel unchallenged from this world to the next, we might say:

"May the waters of life flow through us all as the Spirit of the Holy moves our beloved friend from this place to the next. May she glide on waves of love and find easy passage to the world beyond this one, avoiding any hindrance."

Love flows. Wisdom flows. Life flows eternal.

Water can be symbolized by a chalice, seas shells, or, my favorite—a mirror. It reminds us of the way a lake's quiet surface reflects the beauty of the clouds above it.

# ARCHETYPES, ANCESTORS, GUARDIAN ANGELS, AND TOTEMS

Earlier, I explained that I'm never alone in my rite or ritual. Love is always at the center of my work. I fill my heart with it, open my mind to it, let my body express it, and its spirit is the Holy I so often refer to.

You may call it God, Goddess, All That Is, Divine Presence, or any other name that suits you. It's not the name that's important. It's the difference it brings to what you're doing.

Prayers and intentions can be used to invite Universal Love. We can also bring symbols to the threshold to help others feel the presence of the Holy. A white candle, a religious icon, a statue, flowers, and art can all symbolize Holy Presence.

There are others we can invoke. Ancestors, for example, can connect us with the past and remind us of where we came from. I notice that when I invite my ancestors, I feel grounded and stable. I use old photos and incense and speak the names of those who came before me when I want them to participate.

"I am Ahriana, daughter of Joanne, daughter of Lucille, who is the daughter of Christina, and all who came before her. I call to the women whose blood fills my veins to stand with me at the threshold of change."

Some of us have totem animals, guardian angels, and other guides who've appeared in meditations or dreams and can be called into rites and rituals to support our work. Totem animals come easily to me. (If you've never had the chance to meet a totem animal, here's a link to a free totem animal mediation I created with the help of my friend, the talented composer Armando Olivero: https://www.youtube.com/watch?v=jEiWTa44ug0)

My totems have included wolf, who walks beside me, tarantula, whose energy tingles in my hands during healing work, and giraffe, a being with a huge heart who reminds me to look up and reach for what is deliciously just above my head. She nudges me out of my logical mind and into observation and connection with Spirit.

Most recently, butterfly was gifted to me in a breathwork session. I'm resistant to the clever little being. It seems flighty and unpredictable, fluttering at the whim of a draft rather than self-directing. Yet, as a totem, it gives me an inspiring messages about surrendering to the winds of Spirit and the courage that comes from moving with my vulnerable heart exposed.

At the threshold, you can place fetishes (Native American carvings) on your altar to symbolize the totem energy that feels most important in your rites and rituals.

Many of us are aware of guardian angels who protect and guide us throughout our lives. In one of the most miraculous experiences I've ever had, a healer invoked the Archangel Michael to assist me. I'd had a very traumatic memory emerge and needed help healing. Unfortunately, it was so traumatic that I was violently ill for days before I arrived.

"I call to you, Mik-i-el, Angel of the fiery sword. Wrap your wings around the one called Ahriana and deliver her from fear and pain." Immediately, I felt his wings enfold me. The nausea that plagued me was instantaneously lifted and never returned. I hadn't eaten in days and was so hungry after the healing that I stopped for a cheeseburger on the way home!

Is my imagination opening the way for guides and guardian angels to help and heal? Experience informs my most unequivocal "yes." Imagination is not a just a toy we use to play when we're children. It's a spiritual doorway to a world our physical eyes can't see, but our hearts are inseparable from. When the door opens, the guide I need appears and healing happens.

## SUBTLE BODIES

Human beings are made up of mind, body, heart, and soul. These are often referred to as the *subtle bodies.* In a ceremony, it's helpful to address each of these bodies through our words and actions.

We might engage the *mind* using spoken words or by reading poetry. The *body* will open and receive more quickly when it inhales a fragrance, feels silk, tastes honey, or sees an altar filled with beautiful objects.

The *heart* is moved by inspiring music and familiar mementos that take it back in time, and the *soul* is awakened by the intention of love, which is its true home. You can use each level of your being as a point of access to move you more deeply through the threshold of transformation.

### AN IMPORTANT MESSAGE ABOUT FREE WILL

Please don't attempt to use rites or rituals to change other people's lives unless they've asked for your help.

A Huichol elder once told me, "the only sin is to steal someone else's lessons from them." You can't crawl inside another person's head to find out why they choose the life they lead. Even if their choices seem unhealthy, you must respect free will. Speak words of concern and caution, but do not enact a rite or ritual to change them unless they request it.

If you attempt to impose your will over the will of another, expect a kickback. The cosmic law of free will is not to be ignored. The energy you send out will return to you if it's not welcomed by the person you aimed it at. Angry energy will return angry. Jealous energy will return jealous.

Binding energy will bind you. Unwanted energy of love can lead to a disastrous relationship.

## THE GREATEST TRUTH: YOU ARE ALL YOU NEED

*You're a living altar, made of earth, air, fire, and water, with the blood of your ancestors flowing inside and the breath of Spirit inspiring you. Wherever you are, the Holy is present, and transformation is possible.*

Rites, rituals, and sacred ceremonies are not performances. They're holy portals you can travel through, doorways of change, paths to your greatest potential. The Holy Source of all life is your collaborator in this work, guiding you forward. Wherever you are, no matter your experience level, it all begins with you and your intention. Start with a simple ceremony. Determine what you'd like to shift or change and follow a few basic steps to create a ritual for yourself. Then, do the ritual and notice what shifts for you. Like anything else, the more you practice, the better your rites and rituals will become, and the more effective they will be.

## SEVEN STEPS YOU CAN USE
## TO CREATE A SIMPLE CEREMONY

1.  Once you've set a clear intention, create a threshold. Choose a location. Set up an altar with symbols and icons that fit the work you plan to do. Dress in a way that feels appropriate and engages your body with textures and colors that appeal to you. Take all the time you need and be thoughtful about these steps. The threshold is where transformation occurs. Each step in building it is a living prayer. Take your time and enjoy the creative process. Make it beautiful. Make yourself feel beautiful.

2.  Invoke or "call in" the energies you want to accompany you: The God-of-Your-Knowing, Capital L–Love, your ancestors, your guardian angels, and totem animals. You can do this by speaking a simple and clear decree: "I call Universal Love to this place. Watch over my ceremony and guide me to create the change my heart desires."

3.  Make a Statement of Intention. In your head or out loud, speak exactly what you wish to transform. For example, weddings often start with the words, "We are gathered here today to join these two

people in marriage." It's a clear statement that tells us exactly why we're at the ceremony and what we'll be doing. Whether it's just you, or you and others, make sure the intention is clear to everyone involved. Share your intentions with the people you've invited and the powers you've invoked. For example, "As I cross this threshold, I take myself from emotional pain into the strength of inner healing."

4.  While sitting or standing on the threshold, provide yourself and others with inspiration. You can use music, read a reflection or poem, or share a personal story. This part of the ceremony opens the heart more deeply to the value of the change you're moving through.

5.  Include something experiential. Experience is the work we do to cross the threshold and arrive at a new place in life. Less mind and more heart—this is essential to moving and transforming energy. For example, to release sadness and find peace, you could dance, letting your body feel and express the pain until you arrive at a sense of relief, then play a song you love that brings you joy and dance your happier self into being. You can rattle, sing, chant, walk, exchange gifts with others, do art, bury things, plant seeds, immerse yourself in water, or watch the sunrise. Let your imagination help you find the right activity.

6.  When your rite or ritual is complete, proclaim what has changed. "I now pronounce you husband and wife" is one of the proclamations we've all heard. Here are some examples of others:

    "I proclaim this house a home and welcome you to this lovely place where you'll grow in wisdom and beauty together."

    "I honor this day of my 50th year, knowing that abundant peace travels with me as I cross this threshold."

    "My child-heart is healed. I welcome the little one who's been residing unnoticed inside me into my adult life."

    These proclamations announce a change as though it's been accomplished. Your mind will grab these concepts and move you toward whatever you proclaim as true.

7.  And after the proclamation, offer thanks. Gratitude is how we close the threshold once we're on the other side. Thank the others if any others are present. Ask the ancestors, guides, and totems to return to their unseen realms and thank them for the gifts they brought to

help you. Be sincere. Thank Divine Presence, in whatever form you invoked, for the gift of Love.

Your rite or ritual is complete. When you feel ready, carefully disassemble the threshold you built and move forward with your life, knowing you, or those you serve, have been transformed.

## A WORD ABOUT "KNOWING"

We're human. Doubt is a condition of our being. Through ceremonial practice and self-discipline, we grow confident in our ability to change our lives and the lives of others. I encourage you to take control of your questioning mind. The body and heart are sensitive to change. The mind is usually the last to buy in. Your thoughts are not you. They're simply thoughts. Notice them and let them pass. When you wonder about the changes you've implemented through rites and rituals, allow curiosity to turn you toward evidence that change is happening. Ceremonial outcomes can be immediate or can occur over time. The second is true more often than the first. Transformation happens through our attention to change and our continued intention to transform.

## IT WORKED FOR THEM; IT WILL WORK FOR YOU

Rites and rituals transform people and situations. So rather than just take my word for it, read the stories in the following pages. Teachers and preachers, cowgirls and healers, entrepreneurs, and everyday people tell intimate tales of ceremonial transformation.

At the end of each story, you'll find a simple ceremony you can adapt for yourself. You'll also find contact information so you can reach out to the authors and seek their personal insights and support. It's rare in today's world to be given such access. So please take time to get to know them. They're some of the most warm-hearted and wonderful people I've ever encountered – and I'm deeply grateful for the opportunity to lift them up up so the world can be changed in powerful and positive ways through their gifts.

# PART TWO

## STORIES OF
## TRANSFORMATION

BY OUR FEATURED AUTHORS

# CHAPTER 4

# CAN I GET A WITNESS?

## ALLOWING RITUAL
## TO FOSTER HUMAN CONNECTION

Kelli Murbach, CTRC, MSW

## MY STORY

How often do you walk through the world feeling unseen? In all the chaos of making a life, many of us enter and leave rooms without being noticed. No one sees our moments of struggle as the cereal aisle overwhelms us, or when we correct an internalized negative thought, or when we rewrite some part of our story to become more whole. So much of the work we do remains unrecognized; for me, that's where rites and rituals come in.

Rite and ritual work offers the possibility of creating a safe space that allows room for us to do our inner work while being energetically held by those we accept into the ritual space. I first experienced a ritual providing a space of energetic holding the third time I went to the mountains for a retreat. During a weekend full of learning new ways to support the people in our lives while honoring our own lives, on Saturday night, there was this time blocked out on the schedule for "Ritual."

The ritual portion never earned a fancy name in the five years I participated in this retreat. It did, however, always seem to evoke feelings of trepidation and uncertainty, including *What is this ritual thing? How do*

*I appropriately show up in this space? What am I supposed to do? How will I manage to screw this up?* I could see those thoughts rolling around in my head, and occasionally, someone would actually say them out loud.

I spent the first two rituals I did with this group working through angst around the "you can only offer prayer and worship this way" teachings of my childhood. I'd like to say there was some significant logical moment that helped me through this piece, but I think it was straightforward in the end.

The internal fear said, "Well, that didn't kill me, and things aren't objectively worse."

Then the skeptic chimed in with a "Yeah, maybe they were wrong. And actually, something small shifted last time."

And then, my internal pragmatic showed up and said, "Well, I guess we'll keep trying that thing and see what happens." Once I cleared the lessons from childhood hurdles, I began the journey.

As we sat around the rustic wooden table for dinner, we began our preparation for the ritual. The basic directions for entering ritual space are provided, and we learn it's a release ritual. Apparently, the specifics around the form are still being worked out.

"What happens if nothing comes to us?" Carolyn asks. It's her first ritual of this type, and the question is expected.

"I often consider what I might release during the setup time," someone says.

"You can just hold space if that feels more comfortable to you," Talina reminds us.

And, because I rarely fail to add two cents if I have them, I say, "I never know what I'm going to release or pick up. I just know it'll come in the moment." A few heads nod, and the conversation drifts toward post-ritual hot tub plans.

As dinner ends, Talina and Herb head off to prepare the space while the rest of us clean up dinner and lounge around, waiting for the invitation. Soon, Herb returns, saying, "The ritual space is ready. Come on down."

Entering ritual space challenges me every time. This evening, I stumbled down the hill, nearly face-planting on the asphalt. The leather strips of my sandals dug into my big toe as I leaned toward the bottom of the hill. My heart pounded in my ears, and an inner monologue told me: *You don't know what you're bloody doing. How on earth can you let go of something you can't identify, dumbass.* All the way to the door of the lower cabin.

*Walking toward ritual.*
*Silencing the thought direction.*
*Focus on the moving.*
*Focus on the breathing.*
*Stop before entering the space.*

*Flick off sandals.*
*Plant my feet.*
*Ask the question.*
*How did I want to enter the space?*
*Decide.*

*Open.*
*Put it in my body.*
*Move the feet out.*
*Rotate the shoulders back.*
*Lift the chin.*
*Pull the strays out the top of my head.*
*Breathe.*

Finally, my brain quieted. I stood on the cabin porch, shoulders back, head straight, eyes closed. Listening to the murmurs around me, feeling the wind ruffle my hair, and breathing deeply. Settled, I entered the cabin.

*Let others pass.*
*Breathe.*
*Lift the right foot.*
*Slide out.*
*Point the toes.*
*Angle the foot down.*
*Toes.*
*Ball.*
*Heel.*
*Turn and pass through the door.*
*Stop to be cleaned by the smoke.*

*Find a seat near the geometric center.*
*Look out at the fading light.*
*Listen to instructions.*
*There's no rocks to leave behind.*

*Clench fists.*
*Ask the question.*
*What am I willing to give up?*
*Pass on the first thought.*

As I passed on the first thought, my heart sped up, the discouraging voices in my head stirred, and I felt lost without a rock to hold on to. I embraced this discomfort, hoping something quiet that needed to be heard could find its voice.

*Ask the question.*
*What word is blocking integration?*
*Unworthy.*
*Swear.*
*Yes, that's it.*

*There's a root.*
*Unworthy. Loosely covered by fat.*
*Unworthy. Loosely shaded by short.*
*Unworthy. Loosely held by pretty.*
*Unworthy. Anchored in disease.*

*Tears.*
*Phlegm.*
*Don't open fists.*
*Hold on to the root.*

The internal swearing in these moments shouldn't be underestimated. Letting go of foundational pieces of how we understand ourselves combines to become a scary and necessary insistent drumbeat. Over the years, I've released many more pieces and parts of how feeling unworthy shapes my life, but this ritual collected the first pebble.

*Sit with it.*
*Ask the next question.*

*What do I pick up?*
*Whine because it's hard.*
*Breathe.*
*Find it.*

*Ask the last question.*
*Will I do it?*
*Yes.*
*Stand.*
*Lift the right foot.*
*Slide out.*

*Point the toes.*
*Angle the foot down.*
*Toes.*
*Ball.*
*Heel.*
*Repeat.*

*Let it go.*
*Let it go.*
*Let it go.*

*Select rock.*
*State intentions.*

*I choose to let go of the idea that this body is unworthy.*

*I choose to make this body my home.*

Those lines look short, easy, and glib in poetry. The moment felt so different.

I walked to Talina, head bowed and overly focused on my feet. The weight of these choices bent my shoulders and unsettled my stomach. With warm eyes and outstretched hands, Talina stood in front of me and saw me. I stand there, outwardly frozen.

*Oh, shit. If I say these things aloud, they become truer. How do I tell this woman I respect that I think my body is unworthy of being on the planet? What does it even mean to make my body a home?*

I tried to firm up my voice, but I could only do so much with tears leaking out. With a small, firm voice between moments of snot sniffing, I said those words aloud to another person. At that moment, both commitments shifted from simply a mental exercise to being tangible. Talina's smile warmed, we hugged, and she dropped an "I'm proud of you" in my ear. I could breathe again, and these moments of struggle eased.

*Return to spot.*
*Hold space.*

*Breathe in.*
*This body is my home.*
*Breathe out.*
*Let there be courage.*
*Hold space.*
*Breathe.*
*This body is my home. Let there be courage.*

*The shale splits into two pieces.*
*This body is my home.*
*Let there be courage.*

I left ritual that night in a daze, wondering just what I'd done. In the quiet moments following the ritual, the thirteen of us offered each other comfort and encouragement. We held space for each other, even as we did our work.

My path would cross Talina's twice more before her death. Each time we shared space, the memory of being seen as I said, "I choose to let go of the idea that this body is unworthy. I choose to make this body my home," buoyed my path toward wholeness. That small moment of ugliness and conviction, received and held with compassion by another, supports and encourages me when I find myself again in the sludge.

In the seven years since that trip to the mountain, ritual spaces have become one of my primary healing spaces. All the people who have willingly witnessed my pain and joy within the ritual space have seen me. So, while I may stride through the airport looking like I'm traveling alone, I carry the memory of their eyes and the sense of their hearts in those moments. I no longer feel quite so invisible.

Irrespective of which role I'm holding within the space, there's power in being specific about what you're letting go, intentional about what you're picking up, and honoring your work to make it this far.

# THE CEREMONY

## A RITUAL OF RELEASING AND SOWING

The ritual framework for those five trips to the mountain is based on Cherokee Native American teachings and passed through the hands and hearts of several white women into this book and likely bears only a passing resemblance to the original ritual. Additionally, the language below is only a suggestion; modify or replace it as appropriate to the needs of your community.

## GATHER

Sage or other botanical for smoke cleansing

Container for ash collection

Lighter/matches

Tibetan chimes or singing bowl

A dish or a bowl filled with water

Hand towels

Small, palm-sized rocks—the number of rocks should exceed the number of participants

Altar cloth and other altar items

Tissues

Trash cans

Music player with speakers

Music set list - cued and ready to go

## PREPARATION

Select a space for the ritual with enough room for all the participants to move around the room. If possible, adjust furniture to provide both open space and nook-like zones for different sensory needs. Deploy several tissue boxes and a few discreet trashcans throughout the room.

Set up the ritual space on a table or bench that allows all the participants easy access to the dish with water, hand towels, and rocks. The altar can be part of this ritual space or in a separate location in the room.

With the ritual space set, cleanse the room by opening a door or window and using smoke or sound to encourage unwanted energies to disperse. I've included sound clearing as an option within this ritual as an alternative for those who find smoke challenging.

With smoke or sound, cleanse the people guiding the ritual. Then, allow time for the guides to ground themselves and set their intentions for the ritual.

## INVITATION

With the ritual space set and the guides ready, you can invite people to join the ritual. An example of the invitation follows:

"I invite you to join us for ritual in the lower cabin. Please leave your cell phones and electronic devices behind if possible. If that isn't possible, turn them to silent and tuck them away. As you make your way to the lower cabin, I invite you to mentally and emotionally prepare to enter sacred space. Take a few moments to release racing or self-deprecating thoughts, acknowledge your emotions with intentional thoughts of appreciation, and orient your body to the here and now.

When you arrive at the cabin, you will be offered the choice of being energetically cleared with either smoke or sound and invited to enter the ritual space. Please do so quietly, finding your spot in the room. Specific instructions for this ritual will be given once we've all gathered."

## OPENING

Once everyone has been energetically cleared and settled into the ritual space, open the space with a welcome and a calling in of the Divine. Include the elements, ancestors, guardians, and guides as appropriate. An example opening follows:

"Good evening, and thank you for joining us. Whether you're here to hold space and witness, or to join us in the activity, know you are welcome and loved. To begin tonight's ritual, I offer this opening prayer:

Oh, Divine beloved, please join us this evening as we gather. Allow us to feel your love and affection for us as we release that which we no longer want to hold and gather that which we want to nourish.

We call upon the guardians of the north. Allow the spirit of the earth to ground tonight's understanding in our lived experiences, even as our ancestors, guardians, and guides support our discoveries and intentions.

We call upon the guardians of the east. Allow the spirit of the water to flow through us, gathering what is no longer needed and releasing it back into the world.

We call upon the guardians of the south. Allow the spirit of the fire to light our intention as we grow from this ritual.

We call upon the guardians of the west. Allow the spirit of the air to carry our convictions to those who see us and walk alongside us.

We thank you all for walking with us this evening. And so, it is."

## INSTRUCTION

With the circle opened, you then provide the ritual instructions. I typically break this down into distinct steps.

"I invite you to resettle into the here and now. Clear your mind and check your grounding if you need to.

For this ritual, I invite you to open yourself up, listen to your internal guidance, and choose something to release tonight. Tonight, what you let go of can be a word, a sense, an attachment, or anything restricting your forward movement. Once you've found that piece, imagine gathering it in your hands. Feel its weight and see the room you've made for yourself to grow.

From an energetic perspective, leaving holes within the field seems unwise as they can easily become places for gunk to gather. So, while holding on to what you're releasing, reconnect to your inner self and find something you want to nourish. Like what you're releasing, this can be anything that'll help you nourish yourselves and grow.

When you've selected both things, I invite you to come forward and place your hands in this water bowl. Take a moment and allow the energy of whatever you're releasing to flow into the water. Internally saying your final goodbyes as you remove your hands from the water. Shake off the excess and dry the last bits on the hand towels beside the dish.

Then you can step over to the rocks and select one. With the rock in hand, allow the energy of what you're going to nourish flow into the rock, creating an energetic reminder of the commitment you're making to yourself today.

Finally, I invite you to step toward one of us guiding this ritual to share what you've let go of and what you're nourishing so that we may have the honor of witnessing your choices and seeing your growth.

After you finish with your guide, find a place to rest and hold space quietly so everyone has the chance to complete the activity."

## HOLDING SPACE

Grounding and remaining oriented to the ritual is the key to these minutes of quiet reflection happening all around you. You may choose to play soft background music during this time. Both silence and sound can be challenging for people completing the activity, so considering the participants' known needs is recommended.

## WITNESSING

When I witness people own their stuff, I focus on fostering a sense of gentle, grounded, and welcoming compassion. Just letting them be. Looking into their eyes if they'll let you, and offer wordless noises and gestures that indicate that you see them.

## CLOSING

After everyone has had a chance to participate, the guides can take a few moments to release and gather if they feel called. Then the guide brings the ritual to a close:

"Thank you all for gathering to witness and participate in this ritual tonight. I will be taking the water you released those energies into and offering it to the ground with our gratitude and thanks, allowing the ground to repurpose that energy for something nourishing and beautiful.

Your time in this circle helps remind us all we do not walk alone.

Oh, Divine beloved, ancestors, guardians, and guides, we thank you for joining us this evening as we let go of something that held us back and embraced something to help us grow. We thank you for your wisdom, companionship, and love as we took these steps along our paths. May this evening mark a new beginning in our journey toward living the lives of our dreams. We invite you to stay if you can and go if you must. And so, it is."

## MODIFICATIONS

The beauty of this ritual is that the task for releasing and the task for sowing can vary. In my five trips to the mountain, this looked different every time. Once, we wrote down what we were releasing and lit it on fire. Another time, we put that energy into a rock and then released the rock into the water. One time, we energetically sowed the intention without a physical object. This ritual easily adjusts to what is available where you are in a given moment.

**Kelli Murbach** is a modern-day Secular Shepherdess, Reclamation Coach, and Celebrant. She believes in the power of stories to move and change us. She has 22 years of experience with the work of healing from the silent trauma of emotional neglect. She's called to create safe and inclusive spaces allowing her clients to find the internal order they're missing so that they may be present and alive to the wonders of life.

Kelli retired from structural engineering four years ago to help others to be seen, to have their truths acknowledged, to honor their choices, and to share in the possibility that tomorrow can be different. As your coach, she'll help you examine your stories, discover where those stories knot up and limit your ability to be present, and how to unsnarl the stories so that you can live in life's flow and meet every moment alive and whole.

As a secular celebrant, Kelli works with you to create an intentional, respectful-yet-whimsical wedding, memorial, funeral, or coming-of-age ceremony to honor your spiritual needs in every way. She's also available to guide rituals like the one above.

Sitting (or standing) with others as they experience their emotions, make significant commitments, or experience personal breakthroughs are Kelli's favorite moments of this work. Whether you need space to do the work necessary to move forward or need someone to hold space while you honor a change in your life, she would love to hear from you to explore making the next steps together.

Connect with Kelli:

On her website: http://secularshepherdess.life/

On Facebook: https://www.facebook.com/SecularShepherdess/

On Instagram: https://www.instagram.com/secularshepherdess/

CHAPTER 5

# A FLOWER
# IN A MUD BOG

## OVERCOMING FAMILY DYSFUNCTION
## WITH RADICAL SELF-LOVE

Susan M. Thompson

Picture me as a five-year-old little girl with blonde ringlets and her daddy's dimples. Now picture me forced roughly into the bathroom by my relative. My little arm is extended up as he instructs me to pleasure him over the sink.

*Doesn't he know I don't like this? Why doesn't he quit when I say no? Is this my fault?* My young mind found no answers.

## MY STORY

Visions of this tall, dark, creepy man haunted me for so long. Memories of the smell of stale alcohol on his breath turned my stomach. I remember a noise he made when he ejaculated, like a grunting from a pig.

Year after year, time after time, my abuse continued. I wasn't safe anywhere. As my body grew, he would massage my nakedness and explain how I was going to develop. "Keep lotion on your breasts," he'd say, "It makes them bigger and softer." I felt embarrassed and uncomfortable. He shamed me with his words.

The incident still vivid in my mind was the hardest one to face, and there were hundreds. My heart raced, and I was sweating and dizzy as he pulled me into the usual bathroom. His voice was low and monotone. As I stood there contemplating my next sexual attack, he showed me a picture he had taken of someone I love very much. She was naked and grasping the shower curtain rod. My heart beat even faster, "She likes it," he said.

Tears ran down my little cheeks at the thought of my loved one enduring the abuse as I had. I would never want her to experience the horror of this man. I knew I could not help her or even talk to her about this secret because he explained, "If you ever tell anyone, they won't believe you, and they'll say it's your fault."

For many years I believed I somehow deserved it. After each assault, this predator forced $20 into my shaking hand and turned me loose.

Everywhere I went, he was there. The barn, garage, his house, my house—all had hidden places he could jump out and pull me into. I felt as though he believed he had ownership of my young body and mind.

I know he would've owned me for the rest of my life if not for the healing powers of spiritual rituals.

As I got older, I could outmaneuver my attacker. By thirteen, I watched for the signs and learned how to scope out his hiding places. The damage was done.

The residual effects left from my horror were like muscle memory. My body craved a secret affair, and my mind craved dysfunction. I was never allowed to develop boundaries around myself like other young women. My attacker once told me, "Men are only going to want you for your body; it's all you have to offer." This belief system led me into a life of promiscuity with men who had no respect for me. I was familiar with the dishonor.

The nightmare of loving someone is something I relive over and over. Two of my five husbands beat me, along with a few I didn't marry. I met a man at a bar one night. He was very attractive and just my type. We spent many nights together, and I was enamored. Weeks later, I found out he was released from prison in the custody of a male guard he was intimate with. This shocked me but didn't bring me to my senses. This same man took me to his sister's house. It didn't take long for me to realize they were all doing drugs and an escort service was their business. I was so afraid but defenseless. No boundaries, remember? The man I was with wanted to do some drugs, but since no one there knew me, the head honcho told him, "You can't have any unless she does some," as he pointed at me. I began to shake as my date took me into the bathroom, set me on the toilet, and shot me up with meth.

My life became one dangerous situation after another. The saddest thing was I took the blame for it. The men I chose to love were sons of bitches, just like my attacker.

I got lucky a few times and created a relationship with a lesser of the evils. Once again, the muscle memory of my abuse came into play, and the need to have a secret affair caused me to cheat. The behavior I exhibited was hurtful, and I was disappointed in my actions. I began my long journey of self-sabotage. My abuser taught me I wasn't important. How I felt about things didn't matter. I was to be used and abused by others and by myself.

At this point in my life, I hated myself and wanted so badly to change. Becoming stronger and developing boundaries seemed like a dream. I was living in Las Vegas when I met the woman who introduced me to spiritual therapy. She was a coworker, but I didn't know her. This woman we shall call Becky noticed the black and blue colors around my right eye. She invited me to lunch, and with compassion I hadn't felt before, she listened to the story of how my husband beat me. She became a lifelong friend and confidant.

Becky's wise words told me, "You need to leave this abusive situation as soon as possible my friend." The two of us packed our sparse belongings in the two broken-down cars we had and moved to Washington State. I was now back home where my injustice began. My assailant relocated to Arizona many years before. The familiar roads, houses, and landmarks brought back frightful memories. The effects were powerful. I woke with a twist in my gut every morning.

One rainy Saturday evening, I went to Becky's house for one of our usual girl talks. There was something new about her demeanor. With stars in her eyes, she began telling me about a native American therapist woman she had met. I listened closely as she described healing ceremonies and guided imagery experiences. Her excited words led me to believe I could benefit from meeting the mystical woman.

With hope in my heart, I scheduled an appointment. The day of, I entered the room apprehensively. The surroundings were adorned with earthy drapings and the smell of eucalyptus and lavender. Assorted dried herbs hung strategically from the colorful ceiling tiles. The sparkle of brilliantly colored gemstones placed around the room caught my attention. *What a new experience for me,* I thought as I settled into the soft overstuffed chair that hugged me.

With the voice of an angel, the weathered woman tossed back her full head of gray hair and spoke. "Can you tell me what it is you need from the universe, my child?"

*Now that's new, what do I need?* This is a question I don't get asked very often. The wonderment of it all was brought to my attention: *I really don't know the answer.*

"Bring in the spirits, perform rituals, show me how to cleanse my body and soul from a lifetime of pain and mistreatment," I begged her.

Our eyes connected, and a soft, sacred, peaceful aura appeared around her. *Is this my imagination running wild?* I think not because I felt comforted and cared for, as if the massive universe had its arms around me. We conversed about my abuse, and for the first time, I felt heard and believed.

"You must reclaim your body."

"I don't know how."

She smiled. "That's why you're here," she said as she began instructing me in the steps I was to perform in the safety of my home.

I reluctantly left her office and returned to my cabin on the ocean shore. My little house, sheltered in the woods of Camano Island, was a comforting place for me. Per her instructions, I gathered all the scented candles and herbs I could find. I dug deep in my bathroom drawer to find natural soaps I'd collected over the years. Step by step, I followed the words of my mystical teacher, placing the candles in my bathroom, lighting them, and adorning my sink area with dried herbs.

What I wanted to accomplish with this work was to cleanse my body and gain self-respect. For so many years, I disrobed and let men have their way with me, no matter their lifestyle or intentions. I considered my body damaged goods and not worthy of respect. As I turned on the hot steaming water in my shower, I removed my clothes, put them neatly in a pile, and stepped into the downpour.

*Ahhhh, so warm.* I felt the water embrace me and reached for the homemade natural lavender soap bar. I gently washed like I did so many times before, but this time it was different. I washed away the memories and effects of my abusive life. I directed my thoughts back to the mystical woman's words and watched as the tainted water circled the drain. It was freeing to see the pain and disrespect of so much horror disappear into the black hole.

As I stepped out of the shower into the soft candle-lit room, I stood naked, feeling a newfound pride. I cupped my hands above the candles gathering the calming scent, and redirected it to my inner thighs and up into my womanhood. I adorned my whole body with healing light and let my mind wander to peaceful, sacred thoughts of healing. I performed this ritual intentionally and with much effort, taking all the time I wanted.

After a while, I could feel that something had shifted in the ritual. I felt different: like I could control when, where, and with whom I shared my vulnerable body and heart. It's hard to find the words to describe all the ways this simple ritual changed my life. I moved toward my future with ownership, and as I went out into the world, I felt I was worthy of true love.

Whenever my conviction weakens and self-doubt creeps in, I perform this ritual again to reclaim my sovereignty and self-respect.

# THE CEREMONY

Here are directions for the simple cleansing ritual that changed my life. This ritual can be done as many times as you like until the violation you've experienced feels cleared. If this is an unfamiliar realm for you, as it was for me, let me begin by explaining that the preparation for this healing and cleansing work will be done in a design of your choosing. I'm simply offering suggestions for you; feel free to create the desired experience.

1. You can prepare your sacred space to be calm, quiet, and non-threatening by incorporating accents that bring you peace and ease. I suggest you create your ceremony in the bathroom. Why? Because your shower can serve as a location for cleansing, an important aspect of this healing ritual.

2.  You may wish to sprinkle leaves and small branches of dried sage or flower petals around the sink area or your shower or tub. This helps to make the space feel sacred and ready for ritual.

3.  The temperature of the room should be warm. I like to think of the comfort I feel near a fireplace on a snowy evening. Perhaps you'll add candles. When I do this, my bathroom is adorned with fragrant flickering flames. As the smell of eucalyptus and bergamot flow deeply into my soul, the journey to self-love begins. To help me see better, I also enjoy the soft, dim light of a small table lamp placed strategically in the corner. Select lighting that brings you comfort.

4.  Place a special bar of soap in the shower–something with a fragrance and texture you love. You'll use this for cleansing any violated body areas.

5.  Incorporate undressing as part of your ceremony. Remove each item of clothing gently and intentionally, laying the items just outside the bathroom door or folded neatly out of sight. Do your best to love your body as you remove each item of clothing. This part of the ceremony can feel very vulnerable. Take your time.

6.  Turn on the shower and let the room fill with steam from the hot water. When you're ready, step into the shower, adjusting the water temperature so it's comfortable for you. I've noticed that as the water pours over me, I quickly begin to relax and find myself transported to a sacred awareness that my body is my own.

7.  With closed eyes, I let myself feel the smooth texture of the handmade soap. I inhale its sweet fragrance and become familiar with it. I lather my hands and begin to cleanse myself. Take time here—cleanse slowly and with care. If tears arise, let them flow. Be intentional about releasing your judgments, pain, and sense of self-rejection.

8.  When you've cleansed all the areas you wish to cleanse, rinse off, allowing the power of water to remove any energy of violation that remains.

9.  Turn off the water. You may want to stay in a meditative state as you air dry, or you may want to use a soft, cozy towel to slowly and lovingly dry your body.

10. As you step out of the shower, breathe in the beauty of the room around you. Feel yourself transformed. Bring awareness of change and healing into the room through your heart and mind. I like to cup my palms over the shimmering light of the candles to move the healing light to any place that needs extra attention. My private area hasn't been so private for most of my life. The anointing of candlelight on my inner thighs and into my female parts brings me the feeling of ownership. I am a temple now, cleansed of all abuse and disrespect.

11. When the ceremony is complete, extinguish the candles and rest quietly for a while. You can clean things up in the bathroom a little later. Take time to let the healing energy penetrate your whole being.

 **Susan M. Thompson** is best known by her friends and family as "the life of the party." Although she does not identify as an author yet, she definitely has many stories to tell. With the help of her sister Ahriana Platten, she may claim the title "author" and publish more of the many facets of her amazing life.

Susan's most memorable accomplishment so far was founding a 501(c)(3) in Kalispell, Montana, called *The Little Bitty Ranch.* An interactive animal education organization, the ranch offered community members the opportunity to play and learn outside together. Adults supervised and guided a volunteer staff of at-risk children. The ranch gave them a place to call their own and people they could trust. Each day brought families, school groups, and elderly visitors to the gates.

Susan's relationships with people are something she treasures, and her motto in life is to make the world a better place because she is in it. Because human relationships were once complicated, she has a fondness for animals of any kind. Neighbors call her Susie Doolittle as they watch her walk down the path with five dogs and two cats following her. Susan owns two horses she adores, who are her best friends.

There were many times Susan was sure that the effects of her childhood sexual abuse would be with her forever. She spent years in therapy, traditional and spiritual. A recent therapist described her this way:

"Patient's strengths include common sense, flexibility, gratitude, help-seeking behaviors, humor, independence, love/kindness, openness, persistence, and social/emotional awareness. I'd definitely say she is healing."

Be on the lookout for more of Susan's stories. Hopefully, they will change your life.

To contact Susan, email: susiethompson1955@gmail.com

# CHAPTER 6

# BIRTH OF A QUEEN

## AN HONORING OF THE SACRED SPACE BETWEEN MOTHER AND CRONE

Rev. Mary Rose Love

"We're gathering; come soon! We're almost ready for you!"

## MY STORY

It's a warm summer afternoon, and I've been camping for four days during summer solstice with a community of friends at a fire festival, with lots of dancing, music, and creative fun. My tent is warm on the early afternoon Hawaiian day, and I'm curious about what will happen. My friend Raquel pops her head into my tent, a bit breathless as if she's been running, and with a silly grin, she does her best to rush me out.

"I'll be there shortly," I laugh. She runs off into the woods, her thick, curly hair bouncing in the soft Hawaiian trade winds. I've just awakened from a nap, feeling rested and content. All I'm wearing is a beautiful lavender and blue sarong loosely tied around my waist. Its abstract shapes are reminiscent of the ocean. I look around my tent, grab a flower headdress, and a couple of scarves for around my neck and shoulders, and think, *what else might I bring?* I slip out of my tent, blink in the sunlight, and my bare breasts tingle in the afternoon air.

*I guess I need to bring only myself!*

Closing my eyes, I center myself, pay attention to the feeling of fun welling up inside of me and slip on simple sandals (we call them 'slippers' in Hawaii), following the path in the woods that Raquel just pranced along. The two scarves around my neck and shoulders flow in the tropical breeze, and I feel like a magical, mythical creature moving through the forest. My posture is tall and proud. I feel beautiful. My hair is uncombed, loose, and wild.

As I follow the path through the jungle, I pause when I have a view of the magnificent Pacific Ocean. The deeper blue of the ocean blends with the softer blueness of the vast sky. A few clouds float by as if they are playing some celestial game. As is my custom, I study the cloud shapes, then remind myself my sisters are waiting for me, and I begin to alternate strolling and skipping along the path. Gratitude feels like a warm ball of light in my solar plexus, radiating from my mid-chest area. My breathing speeds up, and I notice my curiosity has blossomed into excitement.

I walk into a clearing and see the Red Tent. This is literally a tent that is red, but it has much meaning attached to it. I know it well. It's here for women to gather, talk of womanhood, sing, nap, snack, weave dreams, and tell our stories. It's a sacred place where girls and young women learn from older women, and we celebrate the seasons of our womanhood.

The Red Tent is large, yet once about 15 of us wiggle in, we're body to body, with the sunlight streaming through the redness of the tent, casting a very ethereal, pinkish light upon us all. The moment I step inside, I'm greeted with huge smiles and hugs from every single woman in the tent, and a fragrant Hawaiian lei is placed over my head and now encircles my breasts. The scent of the lei is intoxicating. My oldest sister, Thea, naked and gorgeous, sits holding some kind of large hoop, not as large as a hula hoop, but large enough to require the women sitting on either side of her to help hold it as she weaves yarn into it, creating a web that looks much like a Native American dreamcatcher. My curiosity rushes back into my consciousness. Thea's face explodes into a huge smile and laughter as she looks up to catch my gaze.

"The Queen has arrived!" she exclaims. Thea is larger than life in so many ways and has always loved and supported me intensely. Six years older than me, Thea has always been my hero. Raquel, a tiny woman who became my best friend with natural ease when I first moved to Hawaii, sits across the circle from Thea and next to my youngest daughter, Rachel. They have created a throne-like area of plush cushions for me in colors of scarlets and purples. There are flowers, balls of yarn, grapes on plates, cheese and papaya, dragon fruit, and mango. My women friends are fully nude or half naked, laughing and chatting, feeding each other as if from some gorgeous Grecian movie scene. It's a feast for the eyes and senses. I breathe in the scent of palo santo, a sweet wood incense that I find delightful, and notice my whole body has a relaxation response. As my shoulders soften, I plop down and snuggle into my pillow throne.

We laugh and chat and settle in. The chatter fades off, and humming and voice play begins. Our playful vocal sounds eventually turn into singing. Raquel and Thea lead us in chants and songs that are easy to learn, harmonize, and have fun with. We sing, "Woman am I, Spirit am I, I am the infinite within my soul. I have no beginning, and I have no end; all this I know." It's a catchy, upbeat tune that sets the tone. Someone says the men in camp are wondering what we're doing in the Red Tent this afternoon and might show up to join us, and we erupt in laughter again.

Thea holds up the giant dreamcatcher and sets a basket full of colorful yarns in the center of our circle. "And now," she says in the grandest voice she can conjure, "We speak of how we know this dear sister." She nods in my direction and smiles in a way that communicates her constant and unconditional love for me.

She reaches into the basket and chooses a couple of colors of yarns, snipping them in random lengths, plenty long enough to weave into the dreamcatcher. The idea is the hoop will be passed around, and as each woman weaves yarn into it, she speaks of how she first met me, what she loves about me, or tells a funny or touching story of life shared with me. It's a pretty wide-open storytelling field, so I know there are plenty of avenues this conversation could go, from the most tender to perhaps the most embarrassing. I'm ready!

Thea talks about being my overseer when I was a baby and little girl, making sure I had memorable birthdays, and about how she protected me in oh so many ways. It's true; I know in my heart that she did such a good job of being my guardian angel, along with my next oldest sister, Bonita. They did such diligent work making my life pleasant that I didn't even realize how dysfunctional my family of origin was until I was a young woman looking back on it all.

My two older sisters made my childhood delightful, complete with fairies and little miracles of serendipity. Indeed Thea and Bon sheltered me in love, and I stayed a naïve child for as long as possible in our humble mid-western upbringing. Thea then passes the hoop to the next woman, who tells a story or sings a song, reads a poem, or otherwise has a personal message for me. I alternately laugh and cry and slowly realize I've impacted the lives of all of these women.

It's Rachel's turn; my daughter, now almost 20 years old, is a full-grown woman. She speaks of her own childhood and coming of age in a way that deeply moves me. She reads a letter from her sister, my oldest daughter, who has recently moved to Los Angeles and isn't present in the Red Tent today but has written a long and thoughtful letter to me about me, honoring me. I'm reduced to a puddle of emotions, laughing through the tears and adding my own two cents worth of family stories about me. My friend Brighthawk stands up and drums out a brilliant tune and chant for us.

We continue feeding grapes and other fruits to one another, sipping lemonade, and storytelling until the dreamcatcher has been passed all the way around the circle, and each woman has both literally and figuratively added her 'yarn' to it. It's presented to me and will soon occupy a place of honor in my home. Lastly, a letter is read that my dear friend Ahriana, in Colorado, has written to me for this occasion. Brighthawk, our mutual friend, reads it for me. She clears her throat and takes on her unique storytelling voice, which is delightful and compelling. She reads slowly, creating emphasis on Arhiana's words, as only she knows how to do.

"Today is a time created to honor you, Marylove. I wish I could be there personally, but I know your sisters, daughters, and beloved women friends are with you. Many women in your life are also not physically present with you today, but they're holding the same space of love for you as I hold. This ceremony today is your Queening. The traditional triple goddess archetype of the female life cycle includes Maiden (childhood, teenage, and young woman time of life), Mother (fertile and creative years, whether a woman has children or not), and Crone (post-menopausal, wise woman years of life), merely the most well-known phases in a woman's life cycle. A special midlife time called Queen also needs focus and celebration. As you approach 50 years old, your children are now grown and thriving on their own. You seem to be enjoying the height of your career, and I witness you being able to focus and grow into your full potential and self. Rise, Queen, to this sacred station in your life. You deserve every moment of its glory. Continue to make wise decisions and live with kindness and love, as bespeaks you even right down to your name of Love. Welcome, Queen! I love you, Arihana."

We close with another song or two, then skitter off into the woods to our collective tents or bunkhouse to prepare ourselves for community dinner. It has been a magical, memorable ceremony that has set me up to be a woman of purpose and grace to the very best of my ability through my midlife years. I am a Queen. Many years later, I now embrace and embody the Crone archetype, calling in wisdom and a new form of purpose and grace. Yet I remain, forever, a Queen.

# THE CEREMONY

Obviously, my Queening ceremony was very specific to the women and the setting involved. A ceremony can take on many forms, including an intimate gathering of five or fewer women to honor the one entering into this special midlife season. The offer to plan and host such a ceremony can be a gift to a friend or family member upon the approach of a significant birthday or life-changing event that launches her into a new chapter of life.

Queening ceremonies can vary greatly and be done creatively in various settings. Incorporating nature is important, and sitting on the ground seems the most powerful to connect ourselves to the Earth. Having women from all stages of life can add value, such as a nursing baby, a young girl, and preferably women from each decade: 20s, 30s, 40s, etc., with special attention given to inviting the sage older women in our lives.

One ceremony I facilitated on a beach included an elder in her 90s, and we created a comfortable place for her to sit throughout the ceremony. Participation is precious; ask each woman to present a token and a word of advice or thanks to the Queen.

One time we shaved the head of the Queen as she wished to approach this time of her life with great humility. Interview the potential Queen to find out her goals and dreams, ask her what colors, rituals, poems, music, or animal totems are meaningful to her, and try to incorporate them. Keep it simple, and don't try to do too much; it's better to have one focus, such as the dream catcher created in my ceremony or the presentation of tokens to the Queen. Keep it to an hour or so, lest it becomes uncomfortable due to sitting or standing too long, temperatures too chill or hot, or loss of focus due to lengthy speeches.

Props or tools can be helpful and meaningful. Consider gathering around a bonfire, using candles, burning sage or sweetwoods, having cushions in a circle for women to sit upon, or doing ceremony in the light of a full moon. Make it feminine in powerful ways; have a queenly tiara, sash, cape, or staff for the Queen. Create a throne or go deep into the woods dressed as fairies. Be creative and match the personality and intentions of the Queen.

Simple and beautiful is the key to a Queening Ceremony; keep it aesthetically inspiring and allow the Queen to leave with something representing her ceremony. Your imagination is the only limit to how creative and magnificent a Queening can be; go for the stars, and you will surely create a memorable and meaningful event for all involved.

**Mary Rose Love** is an American midwesterner born in Iowa and became a westward pioneer at the age of 20, landing in the front range of the Rockies in Colorado. She lived there for almost 30 years, married and raised four amazing humans, two daughters and two sons, who, as an artist, she considers her masterpieces. As both a Registered Nurse and American Sign Language interpreter, she worked in various settings of life: medical, psychiatric, legal, spiritual, and more.

In 2002, she graduated from The Being There Foundation, now named Colorado Interfaith Seminary, founded by Rev. Ahriana Platten. Mary Rose has conducted hundreds of ceremonies in various communities, with an emphasis on women's life events, Red Tent, and Sacred Fire Circles. She moved to Hawaii in 2002 and has immersed herself and participated in a variety of Hawaiian culture ceremonies. As the matriarch of her family (ohana), she now has six grandchildren (mo'opuna), and many adopted (hanai) family members and lives a purpose-driven life, serving her communities with love and passion. She lives on the Big Island of Hawaii, on the slope of the mountain Mauna Loa, the most active volcano on Earth, living her life in simple honor and respect to the Hawaiian goddess Pele.

# CHAPTER 7

# LIFE AFTER GRIEF

## NO LONGER ALONE

Kat Sparks, NLP Master, Sibylline, Certified Life Coach

My husband took his life by his own hand. But this is not his story; it is mine.

## MY STORY

The Texas heat made breathing difficult. Truth be told, every breath was hard since his death. Everything was a blur of images, condolences, and rituals that blanketed the still-living, like a fog settling in the middle of the night. I no longer knew who I was since my definitions of "me" were wife, partner, lover, and friend. These no longer existed. I was alone. He left me alone in this world.

My friends did their best to help, but they, too, were grieving his sudden death and dealing with so many unspoken questions. The shoulda, woulda, coulda thoughts plagued all of us as we tried to make sense of his senseless act.

*Was there something we could have done? Some secret words that were unspoken that would have changed his mind and wavered his hand?*

Like ripples in a pond, his actions flowed around and through us, forever changing our world.

Loved ones came, circling and sheltering me, making decisions when I could no longer function. The first one to arrive looked so much like my husband that several family members gasped as he made his way around the side house. Later that night, at the dinner after the wake, I grabbed two plates, as was my habit, to fill a plate for my husband while I filled mine. Realizing what I'd done, I froze. My friend also realized a moment before me what my intent was, so he leaned forward and quietly whispered, "I'll have some of the potato salad." May that man be blessed for all his days for knowing what to say and showing grace to me at that moment.

A couple of days later, while walking with another friend, her newborn baby strapped to her chest in a sling, we made our way down old country roads. She held the baby my husband had sung silly songs to just days before. *Was that a month or just six days?* Time had no meaning, and days were a blur. We came upon a crossroads. Unable to decide which path to take, I collapsed into a cross-legged heap. I wanted to curl up in a ball and never move again. Babe held tight; my friend did her best to hunker down and whispered in my ear, "You have to get up." *Up?* I had no sense of what "up" was nor how to put one foot in front of the other. She reached out her hand and, with Herculean strength, pulled me to my feet. Never doubt the strength of a fierce momma and a good friend.

Weeks or months had passed. Rising alone in the morning, unable to surrender to sleep, I sipped my coffee watching the sunrise over the pasture. Horses grazed contently, and the dogs sniffed the grass, learning the stories that occurred during the night. My mother always said, "Suicide is a permanent solution to a temporary problem." This saying echoed in my mind as I struggled to move forward. Now my problem was, *how do I get on with processing this grief and reconstructing a life?*

Joining the club called "widowhood" wasn't a membership card I was willing to carry in my purse like a badge of grief. Getting back to our home in Mexico, to my community and tribe, was necessary. Forging ahead with the help of a few of my friends was needed. I wrote letters to a few select women also grieving life events and asked them to join me on the full of the moon at the waters' edge. A plan had formed in my mind, and my heart surged with hope for the first time in months. The invitations were soon accepted, and the full of the moon was upon us.

We stood in the garden, at the doorway of the unknown. Can this really work? Fear it *would work* overcame the fear it would not. Grief is a cold companion, but he is easy to get used to having around. Twelve women gathered in addition to me. Bare feet tingled on the cold ground, and steam from hot springs rose and shimmered in the night air. Breathing in the fragrant scents of sweet flowers, musky earth, and metallic water, we descended the seven stone steps carved out of the mountainside. The full moon began her journey across the night sky as we descended into the candlelit stone chamber containing a natural pool that felt like returning to the womb.

One by one, as each woman stepped into the waters heated by the depths of the earth, we selected a black stone from the basket on the ledge. Twenty-two candles lined the edge of the hip-deep pool, softly illuminating our sacred circle. In the center stood a stone column supporting the domed roof with seven carved portals, so the beams from the full moon entered the chamber while dancing with the candlelight and steam. Taking our places around the circular chamber, we softly took a collective breath.

Speaking first, I instructed, "Place the stone at your heart and feel the rivers of your grief pour into it." A few sobs were heard around the chamber as we released the heavy burdens we carried. Together we stood, all at once united and no longer alone. "Search the depths of your heart and release the burden of the pain that no longer serves you," I encouraged while meeting each woman's gaze. Tears rained down faces, and wails of grieving reverberated off the stone walls.

Time stood still as anguish filled the circle and poured into the black stones in our hands. Soon the water from the hot springs gushed forth from the wall, sounding as if the earth itself had joined us in grieving.

We grieved fully till the pain in our hearts was emptied into the stones. Over the din of the water, I shouted, "Now place the stone over your third eye, in the center of your forehead, and release all the thoughts of grief that no longer serve you." A woman grieving the death of her newborn son fell to her knees. Her sisters in grief went to her, held her, and helped her back to her feet. She swayed but stood up on shaky legs, a woman on each side ready to catch her if she fell again. I felt my own knees grow weak, my head swooning, causing me to lean upon the stone pillar behind me. The rocks were sharp and scored my skin. *I am punishing myself for his death,* I realized. It was time for those thoughts to stop.

Bracing my legs, I felt my body, half in the hot water, and half above. I poured all the shoulda, woulda, and couldas into the black stone pressed into my brow. I filled the stone with all the guilt of being the one still living, the guilt of not loving him enough to make him want to live, and the guilt I had felt at not being able to save him. I filled that black stone with the grief of a thousand nights alone and the coldness that permeated my soul. Finished with living in the past and thoughts of *what if*, I vowed to remember the reasons I loved my husband and let go of the grief that no longer served me.

As the outpouring into our stones subsided, I carried a small black box around to each woman. "Place the stone carrying your grief into the box and repeat after me." Deep breath, "I have released the grief that no longer serves me into this stone. As it is cast away, I bind it, and may no one find it." Repeated twelve times, I then cast my stone into the box, making my own vow. Our work was done.

Walking the perimeter clockwise, we slowly began circling the chamber while chanting:

> *"The waters of change washed me tonight*
> *The stone is bound, and the moon is bright*
> *Relief be mine, come unto me.*
> *To my sacred self be true, so mote it be."*

Approaching the thermal waters streaming from the wall, we each took a stance under the forceful flow. Our sister to our right stepped forward, lacing fingers, palm to palm, offering support as the water from the source beat upon our backs, purifying us. When the time was right, hands still clasped, we exchanged places—the supported becoming the support. Last in line, I realized there would be no one there to support me, *alone once again*. Bravely, I stepped into the force of the water, bracing myself best as I could against its pounding torrent. I felt a hand take mine and then another placed on my right shoulder. Another took my other hand, and on my left shoulder, I felt a firm grasp. There were more hands on my arms. Each woman had come forward to support me under the pressure of the water. I was not alone. The time had come to be reborn again into a world filled with the promise of a new day.

To the right of the archway, where we entered the chamber, stood a stone tunnel with white walls and glimmering blue water. We could only see a few feet into the blackness. Three stone steps ascended from the ritual circle, leading to the unknown. Fearlessly, each woman ascended the steps, walking slowly forward into the cooler water. A few feet into the tunnel, shimmering light appeared at the end. A sigh of relief could be heard as each woman, in turn, saw the light.

The cool night air mixed with the steam and kissed our skin. We exited, and the stars twinkled above, reminding us of the promise: We are never alone. Each woman joined the others in the much cooler pool, and a sister came forward, gifting each of us a single red rose. All at once, we laughed aloud, a beautiful sound ringing through the night air. Together we stood in bonds of community, a tribe, as we hugged and smiled. Relief was palpable as we rejoiced! A new day arrived as the moon slipped behind the mountain, and the sun took its place in the sky.

The next day I took the sealed box of grief stones to a running stream. Opening the box, I cast the stones into the running water. Ripples spread outward as the stones took their place below the surface. As I cast each one, I chanted, "May the water bind it, and no one find it!" Relief was ours.

# THE CEREMONY

While not everyone has access to a privately rented, candle-lit, hot springs in Mexico, you can recreate a grief release ritual at home anytime you need to let go of grief. Follow these instructions:

Gather a black stone, either from the roadside, woodland path, or polished from a shop.

Bring to your tub a candle, a lighter, bath salts, red rose petals, a small box, and your black stone.

Fill the tub with hot water. While sprinkling in the bath, salts say, "Let the salt of the earth purify the waters to bear the virtue of the great sea."

Sprinkle red rose petals upon the water while saying gratitudes. Give thanks for things small and large in your life. Be thoughtful and present in the moment.

Light your candle, saying, "May this light guide me and protect me."

Breathe in the moment. Notice the scent of the water, salt, rose petals, and your candle. Clear your mind of anything but the smells of the room. Notice the air upon your skin and the feel of the heat of the water as you step gently into the tub. Relax as you slide deep into the water. Feel the heat ease your muscles.

When you're ready and centered in the moment, hold the black stone in your left hand. Place the stone over your heart, and see your heart open with your mind's eye. Let go and release the grief, sadness, and pain into the stone. The black stone is infinite and will absorb all you want to release. Whatever you want to say is okay; just let it flow into the stone. If it takes a moment to begin, that is normal. Stay with it until the barriers break, knowing it is safe to let go, and the stone captures it all. If you want, whisper your deepest grief into the stone. This is your moment. Release till there is nothing left to give.

Now take a deep, cleansing breath. Hold the stone to the middle of your forehead, over your third eye when ready. Visualize your mind opening and let your thoughts flow into the stone. Sometimes this seems like you are inside a black cave, and grief thoughts are tumbling into the blackness of the stone. Go with the flow. There are not any wrong thoughts here; it is your time and space. Let the angry words tumble out, think about the grief, and feed it into the stone.

When your thoughts are empty of grief, and you have searched the recesses of your mind for thoughts that no longer serve you, place the black stone in the box, saying, "I have released the grief that no longer serves me into this stone. As it is cast away, I bind it, and may no one find it." Shut the box and place it beside the tub.

As you ease back into the water, chant three times softly:

*"The waters of change washed me tonight*
*The stone is bound, and the moon is bright.*
*Relief be mine, come unto me.*
*To my sacred self be true, so mote it be."*

When you are ready, release the bath water but be sure to capture the rose petals. Turn on the shower and stand under the hot stream. Brace yourself against the wall and let the water flow, purifying you. Feel any remaining grief flow down the drain. Let the water rejuvenate and fortify your soul.

When you exit the shower, put on a comfy robe or clothes. Step outside to look at the sky. Breathe in the air, noticing the scents it carries. Be in this moment as it is hard won.

As soon as possible, find a stream or any running water (a sewer will do in a pinch) and take your grieving stone still in the box to the water. Open the box and cast the stone as far and as hard as you can into the water. "May no one find it."

You are back in your skin, your heart, and your thoughts. You are in the flow, moving forward knowing there is joy before you.

Any time you feel the need to release grief, fear, anger, or sadness, return to this ritual knowing you will find peace. Grievers are performing this ritual around the world and healing. You are not alone.

**Kat Sparks** is a Ceremonialist, Sibylline, NLP Master, Greenbelt Six Sigma, and Life Coach. She resides in San Miguel de Allende, Mexico, where she helps women reclaim their essence, re-invent their lives, and discover who they want to be through coaching, ceremony, and community. Thinking of moving to San Miguel de Allende, Mexico? Kat can help! Find out more at 3rd Act Travels.

Connect with Kat:

Website: www.3rdActTravels.com

Facebook: https://www.facebook.com/groups/594796142309110

# CHAPTER 8

# FOR YOU WE SING

## OPENING YOUR HEART THROUGH SONG

### Janice Pratt, RYT-500

My path in life has had many branches: Business owner, construction worker, teacher, librarian, children's yoga teacher, yoga therapist, and author. Each of these branches led me to grow different skills, learn to be confident and independent, helped me to be a leader within professions, and taught me to be humble because there is always more to learn. However, none of these paths prepared me for grief's mind-numbing, heart-squeezing power.

## MY STORY

Mom came here because she believed I could change the fates and find a doctor or treatment to bring back her life. Sadly, after consultations, tests, biopsies, radiation, and surgeries, it was painfully obvious change was not in the cards. She was in hospice now, and her time got a little shorter each day.

I got ready for work on a typical day in early June. I was off to teach a kid's yoga class, and songs, poses, and games ran through my head. The morning was a bit off, and I felt a bit scattered.

John called that morning from Afghanistan to talk to my mom. She was dying of lung cancer. He'd been through all the military channels to try and get permission to come home to see his grandmother in her final days, but he was still in Afghanistan instead of Colorado, and the best he could do was a Zoom call. John was Mom's favorite grandchild, and Mom was John's rock. Mom was in her favorite chair, the one we moved from Oklahoma to Colorado three months ago, when she was diagnosed.

This day, she didn't eat. She didn't talk, even to John. "Mum Mum, I'm trying to get home. But you know the army. Nothing is ever quick. They were supposed to decide a week ago, but I still can't get an answer."

Frustration eeked from his voice. "I love you Mum Mum. Try to hang on. I know you can get better." Still, no words came from her. But her eyes were locked on the screen. She heard him, that I was sure of. As I picked up the computer, I saw a tear slide down her cheek.

"Oh, Mom. He'll call back. You'll talk to him soon," I soothed, rubbing her arm. "Can I get you something? Some water? Lunch?" Still no answer, just a faraway look.

I bustled around with this and that, nothing important, and then rushed in to say goodbye for the few hours I'd be teaching class. "Mom, I'm off to work. I'll be. . . "

Something was different. She locked eyes with me. A soft gasp escaped from her lips, almost as if she had been holding her breath. "Oh, mom," I moaned as her chest stilled. Her gaze lost its clarity. She was gone. And with her last breath, the vise of grief squeezed my heart shut.

For weeks, followed by months, that moment replayed in my mind. I hadn't hugged her. I hadn't cried. I didn't even say, "I love you." *How could I not even squeeze out those words to my mom in the last moments of her life? Why couldn't I change her fate?*

For years, I pretended to be okay, but I cried every day in the car on the way to work. I went to yoga. I played with the grandkids. But no matter where I was or who I was with, I just felt sad. Until one day, I found kirtan, a kind of sacred singing that reminded me of a joy I'd experienced as a child—a joy that could lift the weight of grief, note by note.

I grew up in a Catholic family. That's where the singing began. It wasn't a strict form of Catholicism, but we were Catholic enough that we attended church most Sundays. I remember the getting-dressed ritual, the getting-there-on-time ritual, and then the solid ritual of church. My mom set up a clanky metal ironing board in the middle of the living room, steam puffing out of the top of the iron like the "little engine that could." My "Sunday best" dress was pulled lovingly from the closet and then, pleat by pleat, ironed into rigid order.

I remember watching from the spot on the couch I was relegated to. "Sit right there. You don't want to get burned," my mom ordered. I sat in my panties with my hands folded—waiting. When Mom finally inspected the results and was satisfied, she placed the iron out of reach, and I was allowed to move from the couch. "Raise your arms." The dress slid over my arms, buttoned, zipped, and fluffed around my body. "Look," I screeched as I twirled around the living room. "I'm flying!" As I flew the dress around the room, Mom moved on to the patent leather shoes. The white cloth she held went back and forth, swish, swish, swish until the black of the shoes shone. "Come put your shoes on," Mom directed. Bobby socks with lace were worn, and a little white veil was bobby-pinned on top of my head. "There you are! You look beautiful," my mom cooed. "Let's get in the car before you get dirty! We don't want to be late." Mom escorted me to the back seat, buckled me in, and then tap, tap, tapped in her high-heeled shoes to the passenger side of the car. Daddy always drove.

No talking was allowed as we bustled into the church doors and made our way to the second bench from the front. Mom placed me between her and Dad, straightening the folds of my dress, smoothing my hair, and lifting my chin with her finger. "Eyes straight ahead," she whispered. "Jesus is looking for good boys and girls."

We stood, kneeled, and said "Amen" together, and finally, there was singing. This part of the ritual took forever to come and was over way too soon. Singing together seeped into my heart, and each time I experienced it, my heart felt as if it grew, just like the Grinch whose heart grew twice its size!

A few years later, around the age of ten, I joined the Girl Scouts and while the meetings weren't motivating, going off in the woods, sleeping in a sleeping bag under an opened-fronted tent, and running through the woods like a banshee with others, was exhilarating. I was born an only child and was uncertain about what a community other than my family looked like. At camp, we were thrown together and molded into a group. In the morning, we welcomed the day singing, "Mr. Sun, Sun, Mr. Golden Sun, please shine down on me. . ." Our getting ready for activities song was "He's got the whole world in his hands. . ." Our going-to-bed song was "Day is done, gone the sun. . ." But the song that made my heart swell was sung in the soft glow of the campfire. "Kum-ba-ya, my Lord, Kum-ba-ya. Kum-ba-ya, my Lord, Kum-ba-ya, Kum-ba-ya, my Lord, Kum-ba-ya. Oh Lord, Kum-ba-ya." As our voices drifted off at the end of the song, my heart felt too big for my chest—explosively big. I belonged in this place. The song made these my people.

Fast forward a few years, and I was selected to go as one of two Maryland State Representatives to the National Youth Science Camp. Held in West Virginia, it was about as close to heaven as I'd ever been. We stayed in cabins and learned to backpack, rock climb, and kayak. We met astronauts and senators who told us the world of science was at our fingertips and that we could make a difference. We started and ended each day with the John Denver song "Take me home country roads to the place I belong. . ." And belonging to the outdoors is what I connected with. We sat under the stars and listened to the wind in the trees. We waited at dusk for the sound of crickets and for the beaver to emerge from his den. Over a hundred of us learned to listen to the voices of nature.

I walked away from that week in the woods forever changed, no longer craving the busyness of the city; my heart wanted to listen to the cry of nature and found peace in that sound. "Shh," whispered the wind, "Awake," cawed the crow, "Be patient," croaked the frog. This trip to West Virginia started my relationship with nature, and to this day, I start most of my walks or hikes with "Take me home country roads to the place I belong. . ."

Time marched on, and I fell in love and made a family: John, Jessie, Katlin, and Matthew. I divorced. My heart opened with love and broke with failure. Finally, I went looking for healing and found yoga. My very first teacher, Joy, started each class with the simple words, "Let's Connect." We began with three long oms at the beginning of class. That's when my heart remembered what it was missing. Each "om" sent a tiny vibration to my heart that caused hurt, disappointment, missed love, and the grief of loss to fall away. Each "om" vibrated with a connection to something bigger.

"Om-ing" led me to chanting: "Om Shanti, Shanti, Shanti" (Om peace, peace, peace), and I was invited to attend a night of kirtan.

*What the heck is kirtan?*

Singing in a yogic way, I guessed. So, I went. I walked into a softly lit studio and sat at the side of the room near the door in case I needed to make a stealthy exit. At the front of the room was an accordion-looking instrument with a bellows called a harmonium and a blanket. Mike Cohen walked in and sat in front of the instrument. He was a big teddy bear of a guy who smiled like he knew a secret. I smiled too. I guess it was reflex, but it felt like the right thing to do. He placed his fingers on the keys, and his hand on the bellows, and the harmonium sang. "Ooooommmmmm," Mike sang. Other voices joined in. "Ooooommmmm." I joined in, "Ooooommmmm." The sound grew in the small space until the air vibrated with the sound. Then just as gently, the sound faded, and the room filled with a soft silence.

"Notice how you feel right at this moment," Mike softly invited.

"Place a hand on your heart. Notice how this space in the body feels," Mike coached. Tears ran down my face. I hastily brushed them away.

We sang for hours, but when we "om-ed" for the last time, I felt like only minutes had passed. I wobbled to my feet, swaying and unsteady, not sure if I could drive home. I put the blanket away, fumbled for my keys, and dropped them.

*What the heck,* I thought. As I stood up, Mike was right there in front of me with that secretive smile. He steadied me with his hand on my shoulder.

"Thanks for coming. It's a good idea to find a quiet place to sit still for a minute after kirtan. The energy is powerful. It can leave you a bit dizzy, ya know?"

He guided me to the chair. I sat. "Just bring your attention back to this room. Get your feet on the floor. Take a few breaths," he softly said. "Where did you feel the vibrations the most?" he asked. "Right here," I said as I placed my hand on my heart. "Just right here."

I made it home, but I was changed. "Sat Nam" rang in my head, along with "Om Namah Shiva" and a hundred other chants. At times it felt like my mind was so full of chants there wasn't room for other thoughts. And each chant opened my heart a little bit more until one day I realized love was all that was left in there—love for me, and for each day and moment of each day. Love for humanity. Love for my mom. The shift was subtle, deep, and profound.

*How had I lived without this feeling of love for so long?*

I became a kirtan groupie. Where Mike went, I went. Most Saturday nights found me at a kirtan event. A renewal of spirit began each week, almost like an addiction. The spirit would fade and then be renewed. Eventually, I attended a class and learned to play the harmonium, chant for myself, and then chant with others.

When I feel lost, I know spirit is just one chant away. I open my harmonium, play a chord, and let "ommm" start in my throat, vibrate in my head, and settle in my heart. I come home to spirit. My heart has found its true north. I hope you will, too.

# THE CEREMONY

There are many songs and mantras to choose from. Here, I offer a mantra that soothes my heart and makes a difference in my life through the thick and thin that life has often offered.

**Sa Ta Na Ma**

This is a kundalini chant that's been researched quite a bit by the Alzheimer's Foundation. It has been found to have a positive effect on memory and cognitive function. (https://wholesomeresources.com/1862/1862/)

The syllable "Sa" refers to birth. The syllable "Ta" refers to life. The syllable "Na" refers to death. The syllable "ma" refers to rebirth.

In this chant, as you say each syllable, you will touch your thumb to a finger. On Sa, touch your thumb to your pointer finger. On Ta, touch your thumb to your middle finger. On Na, touch your thumb to your ring finger. On Ma, touch your thumb to your pinky finger.

Traditionally, this meditation is done for 11 minutes. You start by chanting out loud, then in a soft voice, then only in your head, and then reversing, chanting softly and then out loud.

It also can be done for three minutes, seven minutes, eleven minutes, or longer.

Start by finding a comfortable seat. You can be in a chair or on the floor, on a blanket or bolster. The key is to find a seat that's comfortable for you to sit in for 11 minutes.

Start by connecting to the Earth. Place your feet firmly on the ground or press your knees, ankles, or sitting bones to the floor. Now think of something you may want to release—something in your life that was born and lived to fruition but doesn't serve you anymore. Imagine that as you chant, you're releasing the energy of this event or situation so it can be reborn into new energy in your life.

You can choose to chant with the recording attached, or you can do this independently without recordings. Both are perfect. It's up to you to decide which is more comfortable for you.

Start the music or begin chanting.

After the allotted time, release the mudra (tapping with the fingers) and place your hands over your heart. Let go. Accept that new energy is coming. Notice how you feel in body, mind, and spirit.

It would also be great to do this practice with family or friends. Notice the difference saying the mantra by yourself and with others has on your experience.

Videos for guidance:

https://www.youtube.com/watch?v=GiKkM9VywzE

https://www.youtube.com/watch?v=EVPunsVXxMw

There are many different mantras in many different traditions. The key is that we offer these mantras or prayers with intention. Intention to connect in some way with our true self and spirit. May the power of the mantra open your heart.

Om

Shanti, Shanti, Shanti

Amen

Shalom

Sat Nam

Amazing Grace How Sweet the Sound

 I've worked with children for the past 30 years in so many different ways. I'm a certified school librarian, a special education teacher, and a certified children's yoga teacher. It's fair to say that children bring me huge amounts of joy. In addition to my work with children, I'm a certified yoga teacher and a yoga therapist. I'm blessed each day to be able to offer the tools of yoga to those who need support. My most recent endeavor is that of an author. I've published one children's book, *Amaleigha and the Big Idea,* with two more coming out in the next six months. These stories aim to empower children to make their dreams come true through positive action. I love to visit schools and bookstores to talk about writing and share these stories.

To connect, you can reach me at: janpr57@gmail.com or at www.omtastic-yoga.com. I would love to hear about your experiences with song and mantra.

# CHAPTER 9

# PERMISSION TO PAUSE

## HOW TO ASK FOR HELP AND SOURCE YOUR OWN GUIDANCE

Dr. Aveen Banich

*It may be that when we no longer know what to do*
*we have come to our real work,*
*and that when we no longer know which way to go*
*we have come to our real journey.*
*The mind that is not baffled is not employed.*
*The impeded stream is the one that sings.*

~ Wendell Berry

## MY STORY

The screen door bangs, and a memory from years ago floods my mind. My youngest son James, age five, is all boy. He wanders in from outside, wearing no shirt, camouflage shorts, a fishing hat, and flip-flops. He carries two enormous sticks he found in the woods out back. He's dirty in that way kids get dirty at the end of a long summer day. His face is stained and sticky from popsicles. His feet are filthy from flinging his flip-flops off and walking barefoot in the grass. Innocently, he asks me for a hammer, some nails, and a sharp knife so he can create a crossbow with those sticks. He doesn't like my answer. As he pleads his case, I lead him to the bath, and that wonderful water soothes him as it removes the layers of grime. I smile and remember: there is magic in ordinary days.

My husband and I have four beautiful kids. Our youngest son, the independent boy in the bath with a love of medieval weapons, was born thirteen years ago by emergency C-section. I walked from a morning seeing patients in my own clinic as an ophthalmologist into my own routine 34-week obstetric appointment. There, time slowed for me. I can still remember every detail of that exam room and the following moments. As the nurse placed the ultrasound wand on my belly, she looked agitated as she at first could not find his heartbeat. She frantically moved the wand around my belly looking confused when she eventually located a weak heartbeat beating much too slow for a baby. She dropped the wand, avoided my gaze, and quickly said, "I need to get the doctor right now." Panic set in as she ran out of the room, slamming the exam door behind her. As a physician, I knew just enough medical information to ask questions that would leave me truly terrified. *Would he survive? How long had his heartbeat been so slow and weak? Had he been deprived of oxygen for weeks? Would he be paralyzed? Was it somehow my fault?* The minutes between hearing his weak heartbeat and having an emergency delivery expanded before me—an ocean of unanswered questions. There was magic in that day too, but it was more than ordinary.

In the years before, the idea of pausing my life as a spiritual practice was not in my awareness. The quest to balance my surgical career with motherhood seemed to take all of my energy. The metaphor of my life as a beautiful old ship with billowy white sails and polished wood made sense to me then. I could navigate the seas and move forward when everything was going well. I was unsure where I was heading, but I felt a strong need to keep moving. On smooth days, movement gave me a sense of accomplishment. On rough days, movement gave me an excuse to avoid the larger, difficult questions floating just beneath the surface. Pausing to question my life choices felt dangerous in those days. *Was I trying to balance too much? How long could I keep up this pace? Was this frenetic way of life worth it?*

When rough seas hit, my life as that ship instantly spiraled into a state of upheaval and stress. During that period of my life, it was either blue skies or stormy weather. The line between the two could be breached by any number of work-life balance issues: a child with strep throat or a 3

AM fever, a holiday school program during a scheduled clinic day, or a complicated surgery. Unexpected events, either stressful or wonderful, caused me to batten down the hatches and launch into crisis mode.

I constantly felt stressed, tired, and overwhelmed. This outlook took a toll on my physical health. My sleep habits were abysmal. Migraine headaches plagued me. In focusing on my endless to-do list, my life was whizzing by me, and I barely noticed. Does this way of living sound at all familiar to you? Perhaps you feel as if you do not have the luxury of admitting that aspects of your life are simply not working. Maybe just by admitting it, you feel your stress level rising. After all, who willingly wants to face an impending breakdown that'll surely interfere with your next scheduled activity? I've been there!

If we don't take time to pause and consciously participate in charting the true course of our life, the universe may very well seek us out and send our ship headlong into a hurricane. Back in that exam room on the day of our son James' birth, my ship slowed, and stillness came rushing in to almost suffocate me. In the last chaotic moments before I was rushed into a crash Caesarean section, James' heartbeat slowed and weakened to the point that everyone in that room feared the worst. I saw nurses exchanging worried glances with one another as a "Code Blue" was announced over the loudspeaker, and I realized in horror that it was for my room. The first magical moment of that day was that although he was born too soon, James was alive! Once born, James was intubated and placed on a ventilator, as his lungs were not yet developed. He was then flown by helicopter to a tertiary care hospital hours away. My husband raced by car to be with him.

In the deafening silence of my hospital room that night—the room where I'd need to recover for days before I could join my baby, a true lack of control hit me hard in the gut. Now you might think that by the arrival of my fourth child, no matter the circumstances, I'd have already relinquished any sense of control over my life. After all, on any given day, we have a "laundry mountain" in our home. However, I had lists, plans, charts, and maps of how my life was supposed to play out, and I tenaciously clung to the belief that I was in control. Those unnaturally still moments began to dissolve that illusion. James' birth was totally out of my control. His medical care was now happening in another state. As I was recovering from major surgery, caring for my older children and our home was also completely out of my control. The only thing under my control at that moment was my attitude toward the situation.

I'd love to say I rose to the occasion like some heroic character from an inspiring novel. My dear family and friends sure did. Instead, I fell apart. I was wracked with fear, guilt, and sadness at how it all transpired. *Did I do something wrong? Did I ignore some signs? Did I work too hard and somehow bring this on?* In the months after my son was born, I suffered from anxiety and post-traumatic stress. After six long weeks in the neonatal intensive care unit, James was sent home on a heart rate monitor. The high-pitched beeping from that monitor triggered such stress in my body when it alarmed at home; I don't think I slept more than a few minutes at a time for several months.

Our son James, like many premature kids, had a tough first year but soon bloomed like a flower. For his outstanding medical care, I'm truly thankful. For his life and his health, I'm ever grateful. And still, the experience did cause me to lose my footing—my ship veered way off course. To this day, I cannot explain the mysterious circumstances surrounding James' birth: why his heart slowed and almost stopped the exact moment I arrived for my routine OB visit; how, after an hour (or much longer) with an extremely low heart rate, he had no signs of oxygen deprivation; even how the sky was clear that February afternoon during an otherwise extremely snowy Wisconsin winter allowing for the helicopter to fly and transport him to the life-saving medical care he needed.

My awakening, as I have come to think of it, occurred about a year after James was born. He was finally healthy and thriving, but I found it nearly impossible to return to the status quo as I had lived for so many years before his arrival. As a physician, I still couldn't medically reconcile how he appeared so healthy despite the circumstances around his birth. This uncertainty gnawed at me. I was also struggling with keeping things afloat at work and home.

The idea of taking a break from work seemed necessary, yet it terrified me. I viewed stepping off the stress-laden path of my own making as a huge failure. My ego screamed and resisted. *Don't jump ship.* I found myself conflicted and disappointed in myself. *Why can't I do it all anymore? What am I so afraid of anyway?* My identity those days was so tightly wound in my role as a physician that stepping off the path, even in the name of self-preservation and healing, felt like death to me.

After wavering for months and staying in this energy of confusion, my physical health began to deteriorate quickly. One night at 3 AM, I was woken by pain so intense I thought it would surely kill me. I suffered a terrible gallstone attack that resulted in ascending cholangitis and emergency surgery, and subsequent observation to make sure I wasn't going to require more surgery! I share this because even after the wake-up call of James' birth, I wasn't yet completely on my knees. I kept getting knocked down and then staggered back up and attempted to resume my life as usual. I hadn't surrendered, and my body paid a very high price. I remember my loving (and concerned) husband sitting on the side of my bed in the hospital and taking my hands into his. He looked into my eyes and asked, "How much longer are you going to try and keep this up? Do you need to be struck by lightning before stepping back from work to take some time to heal?" The love and earnestness of his question got through to me and finally helped me to take a break from my clinical work.

We are each being called to grow and transform all of the time. The universe whispers to us initially, but more often than not, we're too busy trying to control our lives to stop and listen. As such, the tougher life experiences are often the only ones that can shake us out of our slumber. Is it possible to reach this level of surrender before a major life crisis or tragedy? If we can pause and connect with those whispers, then the answer is a resounding "YES." The universe is speaking to us in every moment. Why should it take a wallop over the head or an illness to get us to listen? Pausing our programmed everyday life is the catalyst that allows us to seek the doorway within. Practicing the pause in times of relative calm makes finding that doorway so much easier when turbulent times inevitably arrive.

The first step towards breaking out of suffering is letting go of certainty and control. This is the only way to open to possibility. Einstein spoke of how we cannot solve our problems from the same vibrational energy from which they were created. To awaken to the fullness of our being, we must give up the exhausting task of trying to control life. Attempting to control life is in itself a form of suffering. True freedom comes from releasing the need to control and accepting what is.

And so, after decades of molding and squeezing myself into a version of myself that looked a lot like traditional success, I surrendered and allowed myself a pause, a breath, a moment of expansion. My initial pause was dramatic and disruptive and a dismantling of sorts. Yet, in that moment, for the first time since early childhood, I felt free. I heard the call of my soul. I can only describe the pause as the magical moment I took the blinders off and expanded my vision. The pressure to remain the same in the moment became so painful; the pause allowed for a release of pain. I began to have mystical experiences. I felt love as the energy by which we relate to and create the universe. This unexpected trip revealed an entirely new dimension of being. It knocked my ship off course, but in doing so, it helped me remember: we are expressions of the divine. We are conduits of love. We chose to be here. Being human is a privilege. We have forgotten these simple truths, and it's time to remember.

My initial pause shook up my life and changed my trajectory. Other pauses are more incremental, and yet over time, can shift our lives in positive and unexpected ways. The sacred pause will look a little different for everyone and shapeshift at different seasons of our lives. The essence of the pause is stepping out of ordinary time into sacred time, out of mundane space, into sacred space. This act allows us to gain perspective, remember our wholeness, and reconnect with our knowing. The pause is an opening we consciously create within our lives. We pause the stress, worries, and striving, and open ourselves to wisdom. It's a reminder that ordinary days are sacred and that we're worthy of living in alignment and wholeness. In my story, I avoided the pause for way too long. I think part of me resisted because I knew the pause would force me to reckon with some big changes. Perhaps this describes you as you're reading as well. Living out-of-alignment is painful and leads to various physical, emotional, and spiritual ailments. In this way, carving out time for the pause in your life regularly is a profound way to care for your well-being on all levels. Alignment creates coherence. Coherence creates vitality and health.

My initial pause as a spiritual practice was profound, and from that period in my life twelve years ago, the sacred pause has become an invaluable tool. This pause has meant a retreat away from my regular life at times—a weekend away or even a week dedicated to unplugging, breathing, meditating, and deep listening. I try to schedule a longer pause once or twice a year, and I also now facilitate these sacred pauses for others. Equally important, however, is the sacred pause I create within my daily life. This has become the cornerstone of my spiritual practice and has helped me find health and balance in my body, heart, and spirit. I invite you to commit to the sacred pause in your own way and watch how transformational this simple process can be.

# THE CEREMONY

## THE SACRED PAUSE RITUAL

Find a corner of your home and delight in creating a small and simple sacred space. Ideally, this is a space that remains intact between your daily pause and represents a doorway or portal to sacred space and time. This space can be as simple or elaborate as you choose. I find a candle and some fresh flowers to be a beautiful beginning. From there, you may choose to place a photo of your loved ones or a representation of the Divine. I like this space to be minimal yet beautiful.

In my life, the sacred pause is easiest to access in the morning, before my day begins and my children are awake. In this early morning time, the veil is thin, and it's easier to slip into sacred time. Whenever you choose to pause, turn off your cell phone and other distractions.

Light the candle with intention and sit with an upright spine in a comfortable seat.

Place your attention on your breath. Deepen your breath while also slowing it down. Take three to five deep breaths. Next, breathe in slowly for a count of four and exhale slowly for a count of eight. Continue this breath for three to five minutes. This way of breathing will calm the body and mind and remind your nervous system that you are safe.

Next, place attention on your heart center. Visualize a sacred room within your heart space. This is your space and yours alone. Be patient and allow the details of this space to emerge in your awareness. How does this space look? Are there objects in this space that draw your attention? Does it feel familiar? How do you feel in this space? Breathe easily and allow yourself to be comfortable here. There is no sense of rushing or urgency in the pause.

From this heart space, listen for guidance. Notice symbols or words that may arise in your awareness. Notice memories of people and places that may come into your mind. Notice how your body feels, relaxed in the heart and awake in the brain, safe and present.

Linger here, and your ability to linger for longer will come over time. You may want to keep a journal near you as you may feel inspired to write what inspires you in this space. When you receive wisdom, allow it time to make sense for you.

Return to this sacred space within the pause daily and notice how your thoughts and energy level begin to shift. Notice how nourishing it is to step out of your everyday life and into a sacred pause. This powerful and simply daily practice can transform your life. Why not practice the pause today?

**Aveen Banich MD**

Aveen Banich is a board-certified ophthalmologist, spiritual director, certified yoga teacher, and Reiki master. She is also a mother to four children and wife to a funny and patient man. For the past decade, Aveen has been a dynamic facilitator who offers workshops on yoga, meditation, and self-empowerment. Her interest lies in blending contemporary spirituality and integrative healing practices into modern life.

After more than a decade of pushing forward, balancing a high-powered medical career with the demands of motherhood, Aveen realized that though she had crossed many things off her list of goals, her life still felt as if something was missing. Though she had "arrived" by the world's standards, she still felt lost. She craved something more but didn't know what it was.

This is when life became truly interesting. Aveen began to see and hear beyond the reality she had previously known. Her mind and heart were stretched past what she had considered possible as startling visions and imagery overtook her time and time again. These mystical and transformative experiences were, at first, deeply unsettling. Yet as she learned to view these experiences as transmissions of wisdom, teachings that would forever alter how she moved through her world and interacted with others, her life shifted into a daily experience of color, magic, and wonder.

Aveen hosts a weekly podcast entitled "The WholeHearted Healer," where she interviews fascinating people from around the world who are showing up with their whole hearts and making the world better for their presence. She leads ongoing circles online and offers multiple in-person retreats each year. Check out more at her website: www.aveenbanich.com

# CHAPTER 10

# PLACES HOLD POWER

## FROM PTSD TO PEACE, PASSION, AND PURPOSE

Erica Jones, LMT

My face was hot, and my neck pulsed against his squeezing hand. Pain seared in my temple as he crushed my face into the carpet. His screams shattered my silent movie. "Die, die, why won't you die!" My soul drifted up and looking down past his shaking profile, I saw my body still, lifeless. For a time, that was all I remembered.

## MY STORY

Knots tightened in my chest, and dread twisted my stomach as we drove across the invisible border between Nebraska and Colorado in May 2022. Mile by mile, I was approaching a place that held so much pain and trauma. I felt equal parts terror (of facing the reality of what I'd left behind) and awe (at my ability to compartmentalize, avoiding anxiety most days).

Memories raced across my mind like shadows on the loving landscape of our early years in Colorado between 2009 and 2013. David, my love, sat driving beside me. Missing were the dark and painful years I spent before that with my ex, Bob.

The last time I recall feeling at home in Colorado was June 2012, one of the most beautiful and traumatic weeks of my life. I remember driving across town to bake our daughter's first birthday cake in my friend's air-conditioned kitchen. Our window air-conditioner and oven were unusable after six days of billowing smoke and falling ash from the raging Waldo Canyon fire.

Her first birthday party offered poignant relief. Our haggard friends finally relaxed after a week of hyper-vigilance and neighborhood evacuations, knowing our homes and community were safe. Our kids whooped with glee, soaking adults who neared their reckless squirt-gun fight. The water soothed our souls, and we savored that blissful day.

Two days later were obligatory first birthday photos. David's strong arm gripped my waist, and my too-wide eyes forced back tears. *How is this possible? We're celebrating this child, and I just lost the baby I've been carrying for nine weeks.* I was devastated physically and emotionally by the fire that nearly consumed our town. A new job in Denver snatched us away from Colorado Springs two weeks later.

We said tearful goodbyes to dear friends, Sunday rambles, long hikes with the dogs and kids in tow, impromptu dinners with wine, and wild children running barefoot. In Denver, Daddy left for work in the quiet early morning and returned home long after bedtime. I ached for my community, longed for sleep, and fought hard against my despairing loneliness.

We left Colorado in the rearview a year later, heading for Michigan with new hope for the future and the Xterra filled with gear, girls, and Luna resting her furry nose on my newly pregnant lap.

Now gazing upon the colorful Colorado landscape, for the first time since leaving nine years ago, I let myself remember. Fat tears rolled down my cheeks, and I slowed my breathing, inhaling to the count *1-2-3-4-5,* "Haaaaaaaahhhhh," exhaling, *1-2-3-4-5-6-7.*

"David, I feel like my trauma lives here," I explained. "I don't know if I can face it," I said, still breathing intentionally. *Now that I remember what happened.* "I understand," he whispered, reaching over to squeeze my hand. I spent the rest of the drive remembering, breathing, tapping my foot absently to the radio, and tending to the hungry demands from the backseat.

Approaching Denver, I swallowed down the loneliness I once felt there. In contrast, Denver lit David up like the sun. Every turn held a funny story, a childhood adventure, or a special family memory. I soaked up his joy and let my shadows recede.

Relieved to be back in the car, we navigated familiar mountain passes on our way to the magical hot springs where we married in 2010. *How many adventures did we have a lifetime ago in this place?* I wondered as I glimpsed the stunning vista of Mount Princeton towering over Chalk Creek as we arrived. The girls agreed, gaping in awe.

Our history here runs deep. Our first visit was Labor Day 2009. Our enthralling conversation was as expansive as the road when we discovered this unknown gem. We soaked in the bliss of new love, steaming water, and cool mountain air before making the lazy trek back home, nourished by our first adventure together.

"This place is just so, so. . .perfect!" Our ten-year-old whispered again and again, sighing in bliss as we soaked in the nourishing hot springs water. The stunning mountain landscape was her new "favorite place in the world." *Who could ask for more?* I savored each relaxing moment, watching blonde heads as they hiked up and then flew, squealing, down the waterslide to splash into the steaming pool below.

Swimming in gratitude, I realized this place brought us so much healing. When I met David, I was recently free from a toxic marriage but unaware of the extent of my trauma. His life was marked by childhood trauma and loss. Mount Princeton Hot Springs soothed our wounds and helped us find wholeness together. We forged a new path, eventually creating a family that led us far away from this beautiful, powerful place — still a balm to our souls. Since studying the Inca wisdom tradition, I've developed many powerful, healing relationships with nature-beings like Mount Princeton near my home.

*I am so grateful for this man, our four little mermaids, and the love we share.* Inspired by this realization, my heart beamed with joy. A golden bubble emanated from my body, embracing the majestic mountains and healing waters around me. *I'll make an offering,* I decided, *to give thanks to this sacred land for my blessings, as I've been taught.*

Chilly morning air caressed my skin as I slipped out of our room while everyone was still asleep. A sunflower clutched in my fist, I plucked small stones and gathered wispy flowers as I meandered through the meadow. "Cheers!" I remembered the taste of our champagne wedding toast near the boulder where I stood, the mountain behind as witness. I held the love, joy, and celebration of the past alongside the grief, pain, and frustration of the years since as I gingerly stepped onto the rocky creek bed.

"Ssssshhhh." A sharp breath rushed through clenched teeth as my toes submerged into the icy creek. Wading knee-deep, I balanced in the rushing water and sent my *hoocha* (heavy energy) through my prickly, cold skin. Using all my *munay* (heart and will), I gave my *hoocha,* with love and gratitude, to *Mama Qocha* (mother water). My numb limbs warmed as the sensation of heavy energy dissipated, and the creek returned my gift and filled me with her loving *sami* (the finest living energy or nectar).

The chilly embrace of Chalk Creek made me feel safe and small as a child, and I noticed fatherly Mount Princeton looking on, proud and protective. *Welcome, darling; we've missed you. We see your desire for wholeness and harmony in your marriage. It is coming. We support you.* I emerged from my reverie and placed my offering, following Inca tradition, on the boulder, mindfully arranging flowers and stones into a heart. Satisfied and grateful, I silently returned to the room where my human family was rising.

After breakfast, the girls tumbled downhill, and their little hands gathered rocks as they paused to dip their toes in the channel of hot water cut into the hillside. We explored the meadow, sharing our family history. Delighted, they discovered my flowery offering. They yelped as their feet entered the frigid, sacred waters. We said wistful goodbyes to this special place a few hours later, warm again from another long soak.

My body was soft, and my soul soothed as I reclined and watched the ever-changing landscape roll by. Big drops of rain pelted the windshield and cloaked the road, and my heart, in mist as we neared Colorado Springs. Past and present collided within me as I prepared to face the storm of my life.

Finishing breakfast in Colorado Springs, I wrestled internally while listening to the booming thunder and torrential downpour the next morning. *We can't take the kids out in this weather,* I thought. *We should leave. Do I need to face it?* I bravely announced, "David, I think we should drive by. We won't stay long. The weather isn't nice enough for a hike, and I don't have to make an offering, but I can't leave without going to the place it happened." My heart sank in fear.

We drove past the crimson peaks of Garden of the Gods, and Pikes Peak towered just beyond. Crossing the highway, I directed him to the street where I had lived. I gasped, jaw-dropping in surprise as we passed the entrance to Red Rock Open Space. "I forgot about this place!" *How did I forget Red Rock Open Space?* I racked my brain; *I loved this place. I wandered these stunning, red-hued trails every day. This place saved me.*

We parked in front of a two-story home perched on the mountainside where Bob and I lived in 2009. I recalled fat snowflakes flying into the side door as I ushered in my shivering, snow-covered dog during a blizzard. I opened the door, confused from waking-up downstairs at three in the morning. Remembering, I was flooded with rage. *Luna could have died.* My resentment soared after spending the night sharing blankets and body heat with my pup while he slept, oblivious.

Present me knows why. Closing my eyes, the now-familiar scene from early 2009 plays automatically in my mind as it has, on repeat, since the memory returned in November 2020. Characters assume familiar roles, but the vision no longer sends me into a trembling, sweating spiral. I was lying face-down, knees in my spine, struggling against his weight as I desperately fought to get free. My face was hot, and my neck pulsed against his squeezing hand. Pain seared in my temple as he crushed my face into the carpet. His screams shattered my silent movie. "Die, die, why won't you die!" My soul drifted up, and looking down past his shaking profile, I saw my body still, lifeless.

During a breathwork session, I remembered more. I was surrounded by energetic nature-beings. I recognized Pikes Peak, Garden of the Gods, Red Rock Open Space, Mount Princeton, and Apu Ausangate. They bustled hard at work. Suddenly I saw my body arch as I drew a huge, gasping breath. They murmured angrily: *Good! She's back. It wasn't her time. She still has work to do. Keep him asleep; he'll face what he's done.* Then the memory faded. I watched Luna bark crazily in another out-of-body vision while I lay on the ground. He grabbed her collar and threw her outside into the storm. *She could have died,* I remembered. *I could have died.*

Tears streamed as I tried to reconcile my current 2022 identity with the woman who lived here in 2009. She was fueled by hope but handcuffed by shame, too strong to admit how bad things were, even to herself. "I need to go to Red Rocks now," I said. Without looking back, we traced my morning walks—two blocks down, to the right along the ridge onto the hidden, rusty Contemplation Trail, which looked over the valley, bowing before Pikes Peak.

I grinned in surprise, spotting the log where we had taken our first family Christmas photos. I tipped my head up towards the off-leash dog area past the ridge where I met my best friend when our dogs fell in love, bounding toward each other like a slow-mo love scene. Flooded with love for this place, I was pulled from the shelter of our car. "The lightning stopped, and I have a raincoat. I'm going up there." I told David, "Please wait here with the kids."

I dug through my glovebox and leaped out, armed with orange Tic Tacs, pumpkin seeds, and a pendant, hastily preparing for an impromptu offering. As I walked the red trail, dampened by rain, I caught the fresh scents of pine and sage. I gathered a few purple flowers, a spring of tangy juniper, and strands of silver sage to add to my collection. I found a dry sit-spot on a massive red-rock ledge, with an outcrop above sheltering me from the rain.

I mindfully constructed my offering into a compass on the dusty rock. One arm pointed north to the home where our daughter was born, another west towards Pikes Peak, one south towards Fountain where we first lived together with my best friend, and east to the Red Rocks behind me.

I made a compass to honor each of these places and my soul, which helped me find my way back home to myself.

Finally, I let myself cry. Shaking with sobs, I grieved the woman I was, the pain I suffered, and my long, hard journey to find peace. I wept for the parts of myself I lost and found in this place. I felt a torrent of *hoocha* pour out of me, and I gave it all, with every bit of my love and power, to these nature-beings that saved me from my old life and helped me begin anew.

I released every drop of heaviness from my bones, and my tears slowed with the rain. In *ayni* (sacred reciprocity), I opened myself to receive, and I was flooded with joy, love, and endless happy memories of this place. Now the movie in my mind was one of loyal friends, blissful community, bubbling laughter, babies' first steps, dogs racing free, peace, wonder, and the loving comfort of this place.

Blinking back happy tears, I found my family as the clouds parted. They emerged from the car, and we shared one last adventure, hiking the Contemplation Trail together under an inviting sky. Once again, we shared our history and walked familiar paths, now loved by fresh, new eyes.

My trauma was like a hand held in front of my eyes. It was all I could see. As I looked at the vast and awe-inspiring landscape, I noticed how small my fist now appeared, held at a distance. My trauma still exists, but now it's a small thing compared to the endless love and beauty that surrounds me.

# THE CEREMONY

Nature has a way of putting everything into perspective, making our problems feel small in comparison. Nature can hold us, bring comfort, and help us release our pain. Places hold memories and inspire emotion. Nature-beings like mountains, lakes, and rivers can also be our greatest teachers and healers when we develop a relationship with them.

My lifelong love of nature is more deep and intimate since joining the Global Paqo School in January 2022, where I've learned these sacred Inca traditions. We are taught by twelve Q'ero Paqos, the spiritual guides, healers, and masters of living energy, in their native language Quechua, through a translator. The Q'ero are descendants of the Inca, still living in the high Andes of Peru. They live in *ayni* (sacred reciprocity is foundational to the Inca tradition) with nearby nature-beings, who are family to the Q'ero and offer their unconditional love, support, protection, and wisdom to the people in exchange for their love, devotion, and reverence.

My story and the healing I've experienced would not be possible without the Wiraqocha Foundation, the Global Paqo School, and the precious Paqos. They are living their prophecy by teaching the people of the world to return to right relationship with *Pachamama* (Mother Earth).

## *AYNI* (SACRED RECIPROCITY)

As you give, you're entitled to receive. As you receive, you're inspired to give. We are living *ayni*. Each inhale is a gift of oxygen from *Pachamama*. Every exhale is your gift of carbon dioxide to Mother Earth. I remind myself to live in *ayni* daily with this simple breathing practice.

Inhale, *I am loved.*

Exhale, *I love.*

Repeat often to reawaken this sacred relationship.

## SAMINCHAQUY (ENERGY EXCHANGE)

If you are too full of *hoocha* (heavy energy) it's difficult to receive more *sami* (finest living energy or nectar). *Sami* flows from the stars to the nature-beings, who share it with us. *Hoocha* is food for the Earth. Neither is good or bad, but by practicing giving and receiving, these energies can flow like a river, helping you feel healthier, vibrant, and clear instead of stuck and stagnant. Mother Earth transforms *hoocha* into *sami* just as she digests compost and creates fertile soil. You can practice exchanging *sami* and *hoocha* with the Earth, the cosmos, and all nature-beings. As you practice receiving, you'll expand your capacity to give.

Listen to a guided version of this practice here: https://healingrevolution.substack.com/p/sacred-earth-alchemy-meditation

## OFFERINGS FOR NATURE-BEINGS

Making offerings to nature-beings is like showing affection to a loved one. Instead of a hug or kiss, you might offer a *k'intu* (collection of two to four leaves) with a prayer or greeting.

Giving a gift to honor a birthday, special occasion, or as a thank you is common for humans. It's the same to make a special offering to an *apu* (mountain), *qocha* (body of water), or *ñust'a* (special healing place) that you want to honor or thank.

As a newly initiated *mosoq* (new) *Paqo,* making offerings to nature-beings is becoming a normal part of my life. I turn to them when I need guidance, healing, or support. In *ayni,* it's nice to make an offering with any request.

You might make an offering by visiting your nature-being, or you can do it from your home or yard. Use *k'intus,* flowers, sticks, stones, shells, food, candies, wine, or anything else you want to share. You may lay it directly on the Earth, burn, bury, or float your offering in the water.

You may also want to burn incense, sing, play an instrument, speak with, or send a letter to your nature-being. Let your heart be your guide. You might be surprised at the gifts, love, wisdom, and comfort you receive in return.

**Erica Jones** is a Transformational Coach, Multidimensional Healer, Musician, Author, and Mystic. A passionate explorer and voracious researcher, Erica lives in the intersection between science and spirituality. Her practical, evidence-based approach is a blend of 23 years of professional training and experience, informed by her living connection with the divine.

Clients call her the goddess of understanding. She has a keen ability to translate the wonders of the world, the wisdom of the body, and the whispers of the soul into actionable, aligned steps toward a life of passion and purpose.

Erica believes in a world where stressed and sick are normal; rest, joy, and pleasure are revolutionary. She shares content to fuel your healing journey in her newsletter and podcast, the Healing Revolution. Her mission is to help others alchemize their pain, reconcile their trauma, and reclaim their sovereignty, becoming empowered to heal themselves.

Erica guides healing events, workshops, and seasonal retreats and holds space for communities, groups, and individuals. Her work infuses somatic movement, sound healing, meditation, breathwork, bodywork, intuitive coaching, sacred ceremonies, and soul-aligned strategy.

Erica's background as a massage therapist, health educator, sound healer, somatic practitioner, trauma-informed life and business coach, podcast host, author, and retreat leader has helped clients ranging from Olympic athletes, CEOs, directors of nonprofits, and community leaders, with a focus on helping high-performing women come home to themselves.

She adores wandering the trails with her dog and splashing in the water with her four little mermaids.

Learn more about the Wiraqocha Foundation, the Global Paqo School, and their efforts to support Q'ero communities: https://wiraqochafoundation.org/

Connect with Erica to view her services and upcoming events: www.ericajonesco.com

Explore the Healing Revolution newsletter and podcast: https://healingrevolution.substack.com/

# CHAPTER 11

# THE POWER OF MANIFESTATION

## HOW I ATTRACTED MY SOULMATE

Jana Roselynn Laird, LMT, MTI

Have you ever had so many butterflies in your stomach that you felt nauseous? I have. It happened on a beautiful sunny day in June of 2020, and I knew, despite my nervousness, that I was in the right place at the right time. I pulled up to the coffee shop knowing the man sitting inside *could be* the man of my dreams. *Was this my last first date?*

## MY STORY

"Manifesting can be very tricky," I was told. "You need to be clear about what you want, beyond a shadow of any doubt. Then you must believe in your dream to the point of acting as if it's already come true." I took this advice to heart and gave it my best effort—and this moment was the true test.

I was 38 years old and wanted to meet my partner for life, my ultimate best friend, my person. 2020 was a crazy year. The pandemic changed everything about human interaction. As weeks turned into months, and months into a year, the pandemic gifted us with time—time to think, feel, finally take a break, and breathe, releasing the hustle and bustle of life in a capitalist society. I was video chatting with a handsome man whom I met through a friend. During the lockdown, we were unable to meet in person. Instead, we had time to talk with each other across cyberspace and to get to know each other at a deeper level. Emotions ran high. The future was uncertain, and we grew introspective, revealing more than usual of our core selves. We talked and waited. We waited and talked. Lockdown kept us at arm's distance for way too long.

On that sunny day in June, the anticipation of the moment had been slowly building for over a month. To be honest, it was very rare for me to feel such a strong connection without having had any physical contact or energetic interaction in person. Meeting him was sure to be amazing because although he hadn't grown up in the USA, I already knew we both shared the same desires and philosophies about life.

As I stepped out of my car, my body vibrated with excitement. Doing my best not to stumble, I opened the door to the coffee shop. The strong aroma of perfectly roasted coffee instantly transported me to a cafe in a small village in Ethiopia. For those who don't know, Ethiopia is where coffee originated, and ceremonies centered around coffee are part of daily life. In Ethiopia, great care is given to roasting coffee for family and friends who gather to be part of this daily ritual. The man I was about to meet was from Tigray, Ethiopia.

As the fragrance awakened my senses, I recognized a familiar face gazing at me from across the room. I'd longed to meet him for what seemed to be a lifetime. Walking over to him, I felt a sense of déjà vu. He stood to greet me, and instantaneously I had this strong feeling I'd known him for years. As the feeling washed over me, we smiled at one another in awe.

"I wanted you to have this," he said as he handed me a book we'd discussed in one of the many conversations leading up to this moment. I glanced at the cover. *Biology of Belief* by Bruce Lipton, Ph.D. *Wow, he remembered I wanted to read this book! He really listens to me and values our conversations.* It blew me away how, in that very moment, I felt understood in a way I'd never been understood by a man before.

*There's no way this is real. Is he the one I manifested into my life? Well done! Maybe this is a dream? Wake up! Hmm, nope, I'm awake. Time for the pinch test. Ouch! Okay, this is real. WOW.*

For the next two and a half hours, we talked like old friends reunited after lifetimes apart. No topics were off-limits. The initial connection we made online was reinforced in the ways our souls were connecting in person. At one point, he said, "I feel like I've known you for ten years." Blushing, I replied, "I agree. But how could that be?"

Not ready to say goodbye, we left the coffee shop and went out to dinner. I was dying to try this new restaurant, Streetcar 520. We sat at a table outside to enjoy the cool Colorado night. I couldn't help noticing we seemed to be completely surrounded by couples enjoying date night. They were all at different stages in their relationship, and ours was just beginning. The conversation flowed perfectly, stopping only for each savory bite of our delicious dinner. We were together for hours, but it was still too soon when we had to say goodnight.

Standing near our cars, "You have really surprised me," I said with a smirk. In his beautiful accent, he said, "Really, how so?" "With the strong connection we had over the phone, I wasn't sure what to expect. You are everything you portrayed yourself to be. I appreciate that! That is rare." He smiled and said, "So are you." As he leaned in to kiss me, *I hoped I had just had my last first kiss.*

As I arrived home and closed the garage door, my phone made a jingle noise. *Oh, a text!* It was a message from this incredible man. "Did you make it home okay?" he inquired. Trying not to be too eager, I waited a few moments to reply, "Yes, I made it home. Did you?" "I did," he said. "Thank you. Can I see you tomorrow after work?"

I nearly dropped the phone. I just couldn't believe it. He was checking off all the boxes on my perfect man list! I'm sure you all know exactly what I'm talking about regarding the list we create in this crazy dating world. We all have a list!

I replied to him, "I would love to, and I know just the place!"

Since that day, he's been the center of my world, and we're manifesting the life we've both dreamed of. But life wasn't always a dream.

In 2004, I ended a very abusive and neglectful relationship. I was 22 years old and felt like the shackles and chains placed on me during this relationship were removed. I was ready to find myself again—but I also needed to find a relationship! You see, I grew up in a conservative religious household. Marriage and children were the central themes, and nothing else really mattered. There were strict guidelines for when a young woman should start dating. There was a natural progression from group dates to one-on-one dates and marriage. If you had the desire to go to college, your focus was meeting the right man and maybe graduating with a degree in something that would serve and help the family to function. After that, the focus would be on being the best wife and mother possible. The clock was ticking! I was 22 years old, and in a few years, I was going to expire. So, I had to hurry up.

At that time, online dating was just getting started. It was new and exciting! Since I needed a man to feel complete, I gave it a try. Let's just say it took me many years and many bad relationship experiences to understand that *I* was all I ever needed. I was, and am, enough.

Fast-forward a decade. I lived in Virginia for a long time when suddenly I experienced a very strong intuitive calling to move to Colorado. I knew it was the right thing because every step I took towards this ginormous life change went smoothly, and any steps I took to stay in Virginia were met with resistance.

On my 36th birthday, I closed my business, packed the moving truck, and proceeded to drive cross-country with my best girlfriend, Kacie. Yeah, notice the age! It took me a very long time to not only find myself but to trust in my intuition. Strong-willed or bullheaded? Maybe both.

Moving left me feeling like someone took a beautiful purple bag labeled "Jana's Life," shook it up, and dumped it on the floor. I was given a choice to pick up what was serving me at my highest good, let everything else go, or proceed in a life that continued in old patterns. Needless to say, I let old thoughts and beliefs go.

The energy of Colorado helped me make sense of all the pieces of myself. I let go of the pain of the past and embraced a higher vibration to carry me into my future. One of the many experiences I had once I was settled into my new life was a class taught by my dear friend, Ahriana Platten. In this class, she challenged us to dream big and not hold anything back.

I started doing a daily ritual, which I truly believe with all my heart will help anyone courageous enough to do it. The ritual began with a trip to Barnes & Noble, where I picked out a beautiful journal. Seeing the cover, I knew I was on the way to a bright future filled with love and joy. It was all there in the cover art. Every night, before I went to bed, I wrote an entry as if I was already living my best life with the man of my dreams, and I did this for 30 days.

# THE CEREMONY

Now, remember how I mentioned that *list* earlier? The one we all have? Let's get into that more!

First, you'll need to acquire a journal. Take your time shopping and pick one that feels worthy of your greatest imaginings. If you don't have *the list* written down already (and you probably do), begin thinking about the qualities you'd love to find in the man of your dreams. Envision how each quality makes you feel. Not feeling it? I couldn't either. How do you feel six feet tall, with dark hair, a beautiful smile, and insightful eyes?

Okay, let's do this the other way around. Close your eyes and quiet your mind. Turn on your favorite love song to play in the background. You've just spent the day with the love of your life. Get lost in that vision. How does *that* make you feel? Do you have goosebumps? Do you feel an inner warmth of joy and love? Now hold that image, open your beautiful journal and write everything you can remember about the experience you just envisioned. Imagine you're sharing the story with your best friend. Here is an example:

*We just got back from a day of kayaking on Lake Dillon. The water was so smooth that the ripple from the kayak paddle seemed to travel indefinitely. It was like we were meditating and paddling at the same time. We both soaked in the peace and harmony as we paddled to the center of the lake, where we sat soaking up the sun and having thought-provoking conversations. I've never enjoyed talking with someone so much. He truly listens to me, as if I am about to share the meaning of life. Then he responds with a thought that makes me want to dig deeper into the topic.*

*Now we're heading off to dinner. He looks incredible, sun-kissed, and full of light. And the way he is looking at me, Wow. I hope we can make it through the main course. What a wonderful day!*

*I choose him every day and always! We aren't perfect, but I want to learn and grow with this man for all my days.*

I highly recommend you try this daily ritual for at least 30 days. Each day, sit quietly and imagine an experience with the love of your life. Envision every detail. Notice how you feel. Write those feelings down, describing every luscious moment. You need to feel the energy of what you want to create in your life. Best if you do it right before bed. That way, you have a chance to dream about it. The more time you can spend in that energy, as if you are already living your dream, the better.

This ritual works for anything you're dreaming about or longing for. Not only has it helped me find the man of my dreams, but it also helped me learn to love myself.

*Be on fire with a vision that it has no chance but to manifest.*

~ Hiral Nagda

Courtney DeMatteo is a life coach who helped me understand the barriers that kept me from my dreams. After many tears, I realized I most needed to focus on loving myself. Not just the pieces I'm proud of but all of me: the good, the bad, and the ugly. Once again, I found a journal I loved and felt drawn to write in. This time, I wrote love letters to myself for 30 days. I'd sit in the stillness and imagine what I would be like if I was a person I truly loved. Corny, I know, but it helped. If I was having a bad day, I'd find one good thing that happened and write about that. I'd thank myself for being brave and facing my fears.

Here is an example of a note I wrote on a bad day:

*Dearest Jana,*

*Today sucked. It was rough. Here's one thing I want you to remember. You can make it through anything that comes your way. You are enough. You are intelligent and resourceful. Way to go on not giving up! You are truly a badass. Tomorrow will be better. You can do whatever you put your mind to. If you don't know what you're doing, you have friends to call for help, and there is always the internet. You can find inspiration there, too! Keep envisioning the true you!*

*Forever & always,*

*Jana*

I know this ceremony seems simple, but how much time do you put into a relationship with yourself? Most of us always make sure we're there for those we love, but we may have been neglecting the most important relationship of all—our relationship with ourselves.

*What you think, you create. What you feel, you attract. What you imagine, you become.*"

~ Anonymous

Manifesting works! That visit to the coffee shop *was* my last first date. A few months after our meeting, we got married. I found my ultimate best friend and my greatest teacher. Along the way, I learned to love myself just the way I am. What are you dreaming about? Shoot for the moon, and you will land amongst the stars.

**Jana Roselynn Laird** has been a massage therapist for 15 years and graduated from Utah College of Massage Therapy. She has owned two therapy centers and helped countless clients with injury rehabilitation and chronic pain. Jana also has a passion for education. She created the Massage Mastery Institute, where she helped massage therapists learn new body-saving techniques to help their clients. Jana's intuition is her guide on how to best serve anyone she meets. Everything is filtered through her spiritual connection to the divine. Jana has been a student of Kabbala for 16 years and will continue to search for enlightenment.

Her daily mission is to help make the world a better place for all. When she's not snuggled in the arms of her beloved husband, you'll find her on the floor playing with their enchanting little girl Solara, enjoying a great fantasy book on the beach, or in a cabin in the mountains. Thank you for giving her the space to share her story.

Connect with Jana:

Facebook: facebook.com/jana.roselynn.laird

Podcast: Our Vibe Tribe

Linkedin: linkedin.com/in/jana-roselynn-laird

# CHAPTER 12

# CONSCIOUS PARENTING CEREMONIES

## RAISING THE NEXT GENERATION OF EARTH CENTERED, SPIRITUALLY ALIGNED CHILDREN

Rev. Asherah Allen, C-S.C., Lic. Ac.

## MY STORY

*For some of us, our rites of passage were made of scratching and clawing with tooth and nail at the bottom of the pit of parental and societal abandonment and neglect, searching for the rope of liberation that would lead us to safety. Many of us were marred by the trauma of caregivers with mental illness, drug or alcohol addiction, and having to survive physical, mental, emotional, or even sexual abuse. We strove to find the rites and rituals to heal our souls as we endeavored to raise ourselves and our children in conscious ways filled with the love and care we did not receive enough of when experiencing our formative years. It's for your benefit, my soul warrior family, that I write this chapter. It's for you, my dear daughter, that I devote with gratitude this writing and my life.*

**Blessing Way**—*a celebration ceremony for an expecting mother honoring her journey into motherhood.*

"May you remember that you are a team; it has to work for you both."

My friend whispers in my ear as I feel the warm rose-petal infused water drip down my calves as her strong hands massage my swollen third-trimester feet.

I'm seated in a circle of women. Looking around the room I'm struck by the enormous sense of support I have in this community. Tenderly, with soft music playing, my feet are washed, my hair stroked, as one by one, each woman comes up and offers her blessing for my transition into becoming a mother. Knowing I'll soon be living a life in service to my child, I gratefully take my turn to deeply receive.

When mothers, especially new mothers, come into parenthood without the emotional, financial, spiritual, physical, medical, communal, societal, and family support they need, everyone suffers. In this moment, there is no suffering. I open my hands and let all the love in. One by one, these dear soul sisters press a beautiful, unique bead they have picked out into my hand. I later string these beads on a long necklace and leave it on my birthing altar, gathering power for when I go into labor.

The pain rips down my spine; *back labor, ugh!* I reach for the birthing necklace made at the birthing way ceremony. As I hold each bead, I work my way around the necklace, as I would if I were doing Japa on a Mala, and I'm filled with a strength I couldn't access before. I feel the presence and power of each woman—her words of wisdom and encouragement—and the pain becomes bearable.

My daughter is born, and it's the great stream of divine feminine love and wisdom that nourished me into this moment. I look at the belly cast done a few weeks before my birthing way. As I rock my baby's warm body against my bosom, hearing the slurping of her nursing, I'm transported back to feeling the warm casting material slathered onto my growing breasts and belly, and the sweet songs sung by members of my spiritual community. I felt beautiful, then and now. Without the celebration of my changing body by the women in my life, I wouldn't have felt the expansion of my body temple was beautiful, or nearly as sacred.

I'm filled with tremendous gratitude for the power of ceremony and community to birth new mothers in healing ways that lead to healthy parenting.

**Saining**—*a Scots word for consecrating, blessing, or protecting*

Hand to hand and heart to heart, we cast the circle. It's time to present my daughter to the elements, her community, family, and friends. She burbles and coos as we present her to the east. A feather fan is waved about her as a beloved says,

"Open to the power of air, power of clear communication, power of thought, and creativity."

We move to the south. Powers of fire. A candle is danced in front of her eyes and we hear the words,

"Open to the power of fire, power of passion, joy, and vision."

We move to the west—the element of water, and she is anointed with water as we hear the words,

"Open to the power of water, power of cleansing, clearing, healing, and blessing."

We move to the north—element of Earth, and a speck of soil is pressed on her tongue as we hear the words,

"Open to the power of Earth, power of the ancestors, of knowledge, and wisdom."

Finally she is held high and presented to Spirit in the power of silence. Her spirit name is said aloud for the first time, a name that will be known to only those gathered here.

At this time, she belongs to us, to the elements, to Earth, and we celebrate her form. When she passes from this world she will be everywhere and become everything. We rejoice and cherish her arrival among her tribe.

**First Moon Ceremony**—*a celebration to mark the onset of menstruation*

My daughter and I are driving over to a much beloved annual gathering in our community.

"Can we go home for a minute? I have to get something."

"Sure," I say to my daughter.

"What did you forget?"

"I didn't forget anything; I just need some pads."

Stammered; I try not to drive the car off the road.

"Of course we can, sweetheart, no problem. Do you have everything you need?"

"Mama, you've been preparing me for this day for years. I'm fine."

As we arrive home and she gets her things, I search the bookshelf quickly for a book on pagan rituals and rites of passage.

*A-ha! Yes, there it is, the chapter on rites of passage for the first moon.* I grab the book, we pile back into the car and are off.

When we arrive, I take a moment to ask my daughter if she'd allow me to conduct a first moon blood ritual for her with women from the community who are present, women who've seen me through the many years of wanting a child, conceiving, birthing, saining and now—gulp—this.

The merchants' area is mercifully full of a vast array of red items, and in no time, we whip together a ritual and decorate a throne draped in red cloth.

As she enters, my daughter is greeted by a room full of these magnificent and powerful women. They circle around her and share wisdom with her as her hair is brushed and she is bedecked with flowers. Her hands and feet are gently washed. The women form a line, standing with legs spread; they form a tunnel and have her crawl through so that she may birth herself into young womanhood. When she arrives out the other end she is led to her throne and it's her time to share her wisdom with us as we listen, share food and drink, and each woman gifts her with a red item to mark her growth.

This is a far cry from my grandmother's first moon. Having never been told of the event, she thought she was bleeding to death. I send the healing of this moment back through my matrilineal lines so that all the women in my family may be healed of the lack of this magic.

**Coming of Age Ritual**—*a ritual or ceremony of separation marking a time of significant change when a young adult acknowledges the circle of family they came from and begins to develop a circle of support of their own*

Having written her letter of intent—my daughter is ready to participate in her coming-of-age ritual. She is primed now to become a more active participant in her community, stepping into young adulthood and asserting more of her independence and autonomy. She spends the night alone in the forest, a chance to feel into her journey leading up to this moment and what awaits her on the other side. In the soft light of morning, she is witnessed in her growth and she is led down to hundreds of her community members singing to her as the sun rises, tears coming down their faces as we all remember her in the womb, as a baby, as a toddler, as a pre-teen, as a teen, and now as a young adult stepping into her power. She is so deeply held and honored. She is witnessed fully. I'm filled with pride and wonder at the miracle of the turning of the wheel of life and the healing power of ritual and of spiritual family.

# THE CEREMONY

Many of us were not raised in spiritually nourishing ways, and learning how to do so for our children can be a steep learning curve. One of the things we can do to heal this is to divinely parent ourselves.

I invite you to find a picture of yourself as a baby or a small child. Set aside a space for an altar for this work. Place a soft cushion to sit on in front of the altar. Take a moment to be still and quiet, and tune into your image as a child looking back at you. What does little you need? Is there a negative thought loop, a limiting belief your child-soul believes is damaging or wounding? Write that belief on a piece of paper and place it next to the photo. An example would be, "I'm not worthy." Now write down the opposite of that belief or statement, i.e., "I am worthy," and place that written statement on the other side of the photo and repeat those healing words looking into the eyes of yourself as a child. Do this as a practice daily until it feels like a true statement all the way down in your bones. Once the healing statement feels true, burn the limiting belief or shred it and bury what remains somewhere you never plan to return.

Take time to talk to your child-soul. Tell them what comes to pass in the years ahead. Tell them how deeply they are loved and will be loved. What was one of your favorite foods as a child? Make that food as an offering to younger you. You may even enjoy eating it with your hands and letting yourself make a joyful mess. Enjoy nourishing your inner child with good food, positive thoughts, and blissful actions. Practice being unconditionally loving toward yourself. This is a lifetime practice, a daily practice. You may keep the photo out on the altar for as long as it feels right and bring it back out whenever you have a need.

In order to parent a child in an Earth-conscious way, we begin by understanding that we're not just on Earth; we are the Earth. There is no separation. Teaching our children how to have an intimate relationship with the Earth is teaching them how to have an intimate relationship with themselves. Beginning these teachings at a young age instills in them the comfort of knowing that even when their parents aren't around, they're held in the arms of the great mother, Gaia, the Earth herself. In Mother Earth, our children can find solace and sustenance whenever they have the need, and we can rest assured, knowing when we're gone, they'll have a force greater than themselves to turn to and have a nourishing and sustained relationship with.

We can introduce our children to the elements of Earth as a way to foster a lasting healing relationship with the sacred. Playing in the dirt, walking barefoot on the morning dew, squishing mud between the toes, stacking stones, and holding rocks are all ways to engage with the element of Earth. For a sense of belonging, we can talk to our children about how the bones of our ancestors, and all life, return to the Earth. We can tell them the history of the place their ancestors are from and what the first religious practices of their indigenous roots were like. By being still and rubbing two stones together, we can listen to the voice of the Earth. Encourage your children to find creative ways to engage with the Earth and watch them grow up to be well grounded individuals.

The whimsical element of air enjoys much satisfaction from our playful engagement. Gather found feathers with your child and display them in lovely vases as you teach them about each bird. Step outside in the early morning and listen to the wind in the trees and the voice of the winged ones. Teach your children to listen to the voice of the air. Invite your child to join you in dancing with the element of air as you light a stick of incense. As we nourish the capacity to listen, we help raise strong communicators.

With a candle lit at bedtime, we can introduce children to the element of fire. Reading a bedtime story by the light of candle or lighting candles at dinner time helps infuse sacredness into the routine of daily living. We can teach our children to write down a wish they have on the Yule log with a marker and watch the log burn during the longest night of the year. This ritual builds appreciation for how fire keeps us warm even in the coldest time of year. Cooking our food over an open fire when camping teaches our children about the nourishing aspects of fire. Inviting our children to write down something that is troubling them that they wish to release, and tossing that paper into the fire, teaches them how to let go of what no longer serves them. They can then gaze for a time into the fire inviting the vision of what will take the place of what they released that will now serve them well. Opening our children to the power of fire feeds their passion, vision, and capacity for transforming their lives.

We're born in the waters of the womb. We cry salty tears. Water sustains our lives and cleanses our souls. When our children are in the bath we can teach them how to wash away the stress and strain of the day. When drinking water, we can teach them how water is life for all beings. We can visit our local wells, lakes, springs, and sources of drinking water and, with our children, make an offering of flower petals or water from our home that we've breathed our gratitude into. Many children are fascinated by learning about the ocean and sea creatures. Holding shells up to their ear and inviting them to listen encourages our children to hear the voice of the water. Teaching our children about water helps nourish emotionally intelligent people.

Teaching our children about spirit is simple. We can talk to our children about how all beings have an indwelling spirit, including the four-leggeds, winged ones, two-leggeds, trees, rocks, wind, and streams. When our children are raised knowing all life and manifestations of life are sacred, they have a deep and abiding respect for everyone and everything. We're much less likely as a people to destroy our environment, persecute each other, or harden around mere differences if we understand that all life is sacred and diverse. Understanding the Spirit of the Earth, we raise children who desire to live their lives, if not devote them entirely, to the preservation and healing of the Earth and, therefore of the world.

Thank you for consciously raising your children in the Spirit of the Earth. Thank you for healing yourself of the childhood wounds so that you too may walk in freedom and love as we all deserve. May we all remember the way of the Earth and create peace at the heart of the world.

**Asherah Allen** is a spiritual counselor and master healer. Her passion is being of service in helping people to live their most soul-aligned, radiantly healthy lives. Asherah maintains a successful in-person and online healing arts practice. Her specialties include custom ritual design and implementation, trauma integration, and pain management. She is a certified spiritual counselor, licensed acupuncturist, Chinese herbalist, licensed massage therapist, certified meditation teacher, and certified grief educator.

As a Reverend, Asherah offers her services in performing marriage ceremonies, burial rites, baby blessings, sacred rituals, and house clearings. A natural intuitive and empath, she is a skilled tarot and oracle card reader.

Her notable institutions of study include the New England School of Acupuncture, Bancroft School of Massage Therapy, and Certification in Grief Education from David Kessler.

Asherah offers her deepest gratitude and respect to her spiritual teachers Deirdre Pulgram-Arthen (executive director) of EarthSpirit and Andras Corban-Arthen (founder and spiritual director), which has served as the inspiration for this chapter. EarthSpirit is a 501(c)(3) non-profit organization founded in 1977, dedicated to the preservation and development of Earth-centered spirituality, culture, and community; focusing on the indigenous traditions of pre-Christian Europe, known collectively as paganism, which has survived to the present day.

Thank you to the loving and pivotal roles that Juniper Talbot, Kristy Wacek, Amanda Brooks-Clemeno, Leona Arthen, and Sarah Stockwell-Arthen, played in birthing me as a mother.

Asherah would like to give thanks for the tremendous love, constant inspiration, and encouragement of her beloved daughter, to whom she dedicates this chapter.

Connect with Asherah:

To learn more about Asherah or to book a service with her, please visit www.awakenedhearthealingarts.com

To enjoy your free mediation gift from Asherah, please visit http://awakenedhearthealingarts.com/resources/

To find out more about the EarthSpirit Community, please visit http://www.earthspirit.com

# CHAPTER 13

# DUMBFEAST

## CONNECTING WITH LOVED ONES BEYOND THE VEIL

Rev. Jessica Trovik NBCT

*"Just a thin veil between this world and that world of beauty and love. Just a thin veil that hides the view of our spirit loved ones."*

~ Gertrude Tooley Buckingham

## MY STORY

Love and awareness radiated through my entire being. I couldn't put words to the transcendent experience. It was quite indescribable, yet at the same time, comfortably familiar. The only sounds were the breaths between us, permeating the circle with feelings of deep connection. This night was sacred—a night of honoring and celebrating with loved ones who passed beyond the veil of this world, and I was there to connect with my grandmother. She'd passed a few months before, leaving a gaping hole in my heart.

When a loved one moves beyond this world, we long to find a way to connect with them. It's entirely possible to do so. The *veil,* sometimes termed a doorway, window, or gate, is a thin, permeable barrier between the material world and the spiritual realm. On the human side of the veil, we experience all our conscious happenstances, the mundane, everyday existence we think of as our waking life. On the other side lies the spiritual world and the underlying forces that drive life, like the moon affecting the ebb and flow of the tide. Communicating with the spirits of the dead involves crossing this metaphorical boundary and merging both sides.

It was Samhain, a religious sabbat originating from an ancient Celtic spiritual tradition. In modern times, Samhain (a Gaelic word pronounced "SAH-win") is usually celebrated from October 31 to November 1 to welcome the last harvest and usher in winter, the dark half of the year. It's a time when the veil between the worlds is thinnest, and communication with our deceased loved ones is more easily accessible. On Samhain night, we know for sure the dead will hear us speak, and maybe even talk back. It's a time to honor death, resurrection, and new beginnings.

I was participating in a *Dumbfeast,* a ceremonial dinner for the ancestors. *Dumb* is another way of saying the dinner includes a time of silence. When dealing with the ancestors, stillness and quiet is essential. It's when the ancestors best communicate.

I participated in previous Dumbfeasts as part of my spiritual practice. I've been a self-proclaimed Unitarian Universalist Pagan for 30 years. Starting in December, eight annual festivals, spaced roughly six to seven weeks apart, are celebrated by Pagans. This cycle is known as the Wheel of the Year. Samhain is the last of the eight sabbats and marks the final harvest festival. On this particular Samhain Dumbfeast, my grandmother, who'd passed in spring, would be joining me.

A circle was cast to create a sacred space, and we turned off all electronics and phones. After a few last instructions, we stopped speaking. Internally, each of us invited our ancestors to join the dinner. Candlelight danced upon a table filled with specially prepared dishes. Each of us brought food our ancestors enjoyed while they were in human form. There were extravagant main courses, decadent desserts, copious amounts of finger foods, and plentiful drinks. Anticipation mixed with a little bit of anxiousness filled the air as we eagerly awaited to feel and *hear* from our loved ones.

As we ate in silence, gratitude flowed through me as I was nourished by the generous assortment of nourishing food and drink. I purposefully ate with the intent of allowing the ancestors to enjoy the feast through my consumption. I was astounded with disbelief when I tried some German Potato salad, and the flavors burst in my mouth so excitingly that I couldn't get enough. Before I knew it, I devoured the entire serving. The flavors brought a profusion of pleasures to my mouth, and I desperately wanted more. It was quite peculiar because previously, I wasn't a fan of German potato salad. I allowed myself to enjoy the dish for someone's ancestor, and clearly, they wanted more! To this day, I still love German potato salad.

I relished other delicacies and felt the presence of the unseen among us. It was a somber yet loving affair, a time to feel the blessing of those we were missing. As those of us in physical form were finishing up the foods that filled our plates, I thought about my grandmother and her passage over the rainbow bridge. Thoughtfully, I started eating the pumpkin pie I had brought specifically for her. I invited her to attend this Dumbfeast with me, and she reminded me that her favorite dessert was pie—any variety of pie. Any kind of sweets was her favorite. The creamy and pungent pumpkin filling filled my mouth with joy. I felt a sense of sadness because I missed her dearly, yet joy because thinking about her always brought a smile to my face.

Suddenly, I could make out the faint smell of roses. It became stronger until I heard, *I'm always with you, Jessie.* The hairs on my arm stood up and the desire to cry overcame me. It was Grandma! She came! Not that I doubted she would, but it had been a long time since I'd been in her presence. I imagined myself wrapped in her arms. Her furry black coat enveloped me in a giant embrace—just like when I was a small child and she swooped me up inside her oversized jacket and bear-hugged me. I couldn't hold back the flow of tears that silently cascaded down my cheeks. I was elated and at the same time so sad because I missed her desperately. The heartache of her passing was still fresh and raw. But she was with me that night and I cherished every minute of it.

Like all things, the dinner eventually came to an end and we had to say our goodbyes, but I knew it wasn't forever. As she said, she's always with me. I have the tools and the means to connect with her whenever I need to, but especially at the time of year when the veils are the thinnest.

I promised her more pie at the next Dumbfeast: *Oh, how I hope there will be more German potato salad,* I secretly thought.

# THE CEREMONY

All over the world, indigenous peoples and cultures honor their deceased loved ones in one way or another. Several native cultures invoke their ancestors daily through ritual. Our ancestors hold great wisdom; they survived and learned before us, and we can invoke and ask them to guide us with that wisdom.

Honoring our deceased loved ones evokes in us a human connection to the natural cycle of life and death. In our mundane life, it's easy to forget, and perhaps even more challenging to accept, that death is a natural part of the wheel of life.

The Dumbfeast is a beautiful ceremony to honor your deceased loved ones and to communicate with them when the veils are thin. There are also several daily rituals you can participate in to remember and honor your friends and family who've died.

Here are several ways, including the Dumbfeast, in which you can celebrate your loved one or loved ones who have passed beyond the veil:

## DUMBFEAST

A traditional Dumbfeast is held on Samhain, or Halloween, the night when the veil between our world and the spirit world is at its most delicate.

Begin by making your dining area ready for the ceremony. You can cast a circle, smudge the area, ring bells, or use some other method of creating sacred space. Turn off your phone and television to eliminate outside distractions. Remember that this is a silent occasion. You may want to make other arrangements for younger children. This ceremony can be difficult for them because it requires them to be quiet.

Each participant who is invited to attend will bring a favorite dish of the loved one or loved ones they're honoring. Set the table with a black cloth, black plates, cutlery, and black napkins. Use candles as your only source of light. Reserve a setting at the table as a place for the ancestors.

Once everyone is seated, silently bless the meal. Give instructions for each person to silently extend an internal invitation to those they wish to invite. When they're done, quietly pass the food around and let each person take what they wish. Begin eating in silence. At some point, someone will feel moved to speak. At this time, guests take turns sharing about their loved ones. Allow time for these sweet stories. When everyone who wants to has shared, the invited ancestors and spirits are thanked for attending and asked to return to where they came from. Sacred space is released, and participants can share the remaining food and drink merrily.

## SETTING A PLACE AT THE TABLE

Save your ancestor a seat at special gatherings and events by setting a place at the table for them. Do this as a daily ritual if you feel inspired. Setting a place at the table can be a reminder of their lasting presence in your life. They're always invited, and you hope they attend in spirit. Saving a place for them reminds everyone of their eternal presence, as well as inspiring memories of past events. Consider serving one of their favorite foods. When you eat their favorite food, imagine you're enjoying it for your loved one.

## CREATING AN ALTAR

In several traditions and cultures, altars are a way to remember loved ones after their death. The creation of altars goes back to the shrines of Ancient Greece and to the Day of the Dead altars in modern Mexico.

Creating an altar is a way to put your feelings and thoughts into the physical world. They help you remember, heal, and reflect. Take your time with this process. Use the moment to connect with your loved one and create something in their honor.

Set up your altar space and make it personal. Add things like:

- Framed photos
- Candles
- Incense
- Bells or chimes
- Symbols
- Rocks or crystals
- Flowers
- Personal objects

## SÉANCES

A séance is one way to communicate with the spiritual world. Seances can be performed at home in several ways and have been said to unlock the key to the ethereal world.

You'll need to decide how you're going to communicate with your loved one. Using objects such as a pendulum or Ouija board is common. It's also helpful to have a photograph of the person you're contacting.

Find a clear space where you can have a table to gather around. You can use incense and candles.

Séances are usually conducted in small groups and involve some form of ritual. A standard method consists of joining hands around a table and chanting. Having several people who are open to the spiritual world will help strengthen your connection with the spirit world and improve your chances of making contact.

It's vital to begin your séance by stating your intention and asking the loved one to make contact. Keeping an open mind and freeing yourself of any expectations can improve your chances of success.

When the séance is complete, it's customary to thank the spirit or spirits and send them back to where they came from.

## MEMORIAL TABLE AT A CEREMONY

Some people create a memorial table at a special ceremony or reception, like a wedding. This table may include pictures of the deceased, beloved items, favorite flowers, and candles. Another way to honor those who have crossed the veil is to pause during the ceremony to light a memorial candle for them.

## QUILT OF CLOTHES

Consider making a quilt out of your deceased loved one's clothes. As you look through their clothing, you need to think about the type of fabrics you choose to put in your quilt. If you select an item that's dry-cleaning only, then what you make out of it will also have to be dry-cleaned. Typically, you can create one quilt block from each item; 30 to 40 items would make a decent-sized quilt.

## MIRROR GAZING

You can use mirror-gazing to see the spirit of your loved one. Mirror gazing goes back to ancient times. The Greeks used mirror gazing to contact departed loved ones. The practice was so prevalent that temples were built to accommodate priestesses who gazed into a cauldron, or a mirror, to deliver messages to relatives.

The best time to mirror gaze is in the evening or at twilight. This is a time when we can easily transition into a slightly altered state of consciousness. Clean and bless your mirror. Stare at the point where your third eye is, which is just above your eyebrows in the middle of your forehead. Now soften your gaze. Keeping your eyes relaxed, gaze at this point for as long as you can. With your peripheral vision, notice any energy waves begin to manifest around your shoulders or head. If you are staring too hard, soften your gaze. Intense staring makes your eyes tire quickly. A relaxed gaze won't strain your eyes. Ask your loved one to visit with you and see what happens. You may feel them with you, or you may hear a message come through. You may also see flickers of light or a vision.

When you finish with your session, clean your mirror and put it away. As an added protection, place a black velvet cloth to cover it when it's not in use.

## LETTER WRITING

Writing a letter to your deceased loved one can be very beneficial and cathartic. Let them know how much you miss and love them. Share secrets. Write about your emotions: Are you angry? Sad? Healing? Let your feelings out on paper. When you've finished writing, read the letter aloud. Then, burn it or bury it.

## TALK TO THEM

One of the easiest ways to get your deceased loved one to communicate with you is just to talk. Just start speaking. Hold an image of the person you're trying to communicate with within your mind and direct your communication to them. Wait patiently to feel or hear their reply.

## TAKE A TRIP

Take that trip your loved one always dreamed of taking or had already been in the process of planning. Imagine they're there with you and experience the sites and adventures they'd enjoy. This is a great way to feel close to your loved one and to experience first-hand the things they would've adored.

## WEAR AN ITEM OF THEIRS

Wearing something that belonged to a loved one is a simple and meaningful tribute to them. Whether it's a wristwatch, a hat, a piece of jewelry, or an article of clothing, you'll have their memory close all day.

## CREATE JEWELRY WITH THEIR HANDWRITING

The unique script of your loved one evokes precious memories. Creating a piece of memorial jewelry that features printed or engraved images of their actual words is a one-of-a-kind reminder of them that you can wear daily.

## FRAME SOMETHING THEY'VE WRITTEN

Seeing something written by your loved one and then framed is something truly unique and special. Consider putting a treasured letter, recipe, or anything else cherished and handwritten in a unique frame. You'll remember your loved one each time you pass it. You could even place the frame on your altar.

## MARK A SPOT IN THEIR HONOR

Sponsoring a plaque, a brick, or a bench at one of their favorite places is a lasting legacy. You could also honor them by planting a tree, flower, or bush in their memory. Whether you choose a tree, a rose bush, or a whole garden, doing some planting in your loved one's honor can help you honor their memory as well. It's their tree or their bush, and whenever you tend to it or see it, you'll think of them. It's gorgeous when the birds and butterflies take shelter in the tree or bush you planted for them.

## MAKE A SCRAPBOOK OF THEIR LIFE

Create a tribute that honors your loved one's life by gathering photos and stories of them to place in a scrapbook. This is a beautiful way to celebrate their legacy and pass it down through the generations.

## GET PERMANENTLY INKED

You might consider getting a tattoo of their name, dates of birth and death, or an image or symbol that meant something to you and your loved one. You could also consider getting a quote written in their handwriting. It honors their memory and won't fade with time.

**Jessica Trovik** has been a teacher for 21 years and is currently a middle school Math teacher in Colorado Springs, Colorado. After graduating with a bachelor's degree in Public Relations from Pepperdine University in 1993, she worked in the service and hotel industries until 2001. She decided to follow her passion for teaching and went through an alternative licensure program to attain her educator license, becoming a National Board-Certified Teacher in 2011. She received her master's degree in Education in 2012 from the University of Colorado. Shortly after that, she finished her doctorate in Sociology. Jessie is an ordained interfaith minister who worked as a young adult coordinator with the Unitarian Universalist Association for seven years, from 2002 to 2009. She's been a practicing pagan for over three decades and has participated in numerous rites and rituals over the years. She and her wife, Danna, enjoy beautiful Colorado outdoors and enjoy camping and playing golf in their spare time.

Connect with Jessie:

Email: jtrovik@gmail.com

Facebook: Jessie Trovik

# CHAPTER 14

# RITUALIZING RELATIONSHIP

## BLESSING THE PAST, THE PRESENT, AND THE FUTURE

Roger Butts

In her seminal book, *Beloved,* Toni Morrison introduced me to the power—heart power, mind power—of sacred ceremony.

## MY STORY

### PART 1: BABY SUGGS

At Wesley Seminary in Washington, DC, I took African American Literature as Spiritual Practice, under the guidance of professor and scholar Josiah Ulysses Young, III. We read W.E.B. Dubois. We read James Baldwin. And we read Toni Morrison's *Beloved.*

We gathered once a week to explore what this literature could mean for us as ministers, and for the churches we'd serve. We were black Baptists and Asian Methodists, feminists, Unitarian Universalists, gay and straight wrestling with what DuBois called the greatest issue facing the American democratic experiment: racism.

We moved along in our reading. We read *The Coming of John,* from W.E.B. Dubois' classic and essential text, *The Soul of Black Folks.* We read James Baldwin's *The Fire Next Time.*

We engaged Baldwin's quotes such as: "Love takes off the masks that we fear we cannot live without and know we cannot live within. I use the word "love" here not merely in the personal sense but as a state of being, or a state of grace - not in the infantile American sense of being made happy but in the tough and universal sense of quest and daring and growth."

And,

"The American Negro has the great advantage of having never believed the collection of myths to which white Americans cling: that their ancestors were all freedom-loving heroes, that they were born in the greatest country the world has ever seen, or that Americans are invincible in battle and wise in peace, that Americans have always dealt honorably with Mexicans and Indians and all other neighbors or inferiors, that American men are the world's most direct and virile, that American women are pure. Negroes know far more about white Americans than that. . .The tendency has really been, insofar as this was possible, to dismiss white people as the slightly mad victims of their own brainwashing."

We struggled together, mining the liberating message we might hear. Then came an explosive moment. Toni Morrison's *Beloved* was the text, and we devoured it. *Beloved* gave us a glimpse into the way slavery and post-slavery deeply and negatively impacted the slaveholders and the enslaved. *Beloved* gave us rich characters who struggled to make meaning of what they experienced in their resilient, powerful community.

It showed us what trauma could do to the imagination and memory and how disorienting it can be. It showed us how memory lives as a vicious character and how hope can be activated in relationships and community— how a mother will go to great lengths to protect her baby, the *Beloved.* Community, betrayal, resilience, imagination, love, memory—they're all explored in this mythical book.

For me, one passage teaches me about sacred ceremony in a way I've rarely experienced in print: Baby Suggs' sermon in the clearing.

Baby Suggs was the matriarch of this community. When warm weather came, she went out to the clearing followed by her whole community. In that place, they were safe. They need not be anything other than who they were, fully, and without any kind of pretense.

In the book, the scene begins with a telling line: *"It was time to lay it all down."* It was time to lay down the pain, the suffering, the frustration, the fear, and the rage. It was time to put away the horror, the dehumanization, the being hunted down like animals.

It was time to put that aside and take up sacred ceremony. It was time to lay all that down through communal, sacred ceremony.

Baby Suggs, without any kind of ordination or formal title, provided a ritual of remembrance, lament, and hope.

Once everyone gathered around, Baby Suggs put down her walking stick and prepared to speak.

And then, Toni Morrison writes, *"Baby Suggs offered up her great big heart."*

This heart offering is the foundation of sacred ceremony. I remind you: It is not head-to-head. It is not intellectual or abstract. It is heart-to-heart. It is the giving and receiving of deep heart space. Trust, love, compassion: connection. What Baby Suggs offered is what all of us who invest ourselves in rites and rituals offer—our great big hearts.

Baby Suggs began the sacred ceremony with a simple invitation. She invited the men to step forward. And all the men came forth. She asked them to dance. At that moment they danced the antelope dance, a dance of virility and power, but even more than that, a dance that reminded the men—and all gathered—of the dance of Mother Africa.

Now in diaspora, now violently displaced, they were remembering. In my recounting of this scene, those gathered said to their enslavers a loud and powerful "No!" They said to the slave owners' religion and politics a powerful "No!" I can imagine them proclaiming: You do not get to define us. This dance is who we are, past, present, and future. This ritual and this community are who we are. Your attempt at defining us will not land. We know who we are, and we remember. And to do so we dance, fully embodied, fully alive.

Baby Suggs then asked the children to come forward. Let your mothers and fathers and all gathered here see you laugh. Laugh. This is a precious part of the ritual. This is the embodiment of joy and hope. This is where the community glimpses its future and holds its dreams for a new world. They know there are no guarantees. They're aware that much is at stake. That can wait. Now is the time to dance and laugh.

Then, Baby Suggs asked all the women to come forth. Cry. Cry for the living and the dead. And the women cried. This is the primal grief of so much lost, the nameless ancestors, the Middle Passage. This is the cry of the forsaken, the cry of the oppressed.

In sermons all over, this is the kind of cry of injustice and grief that preachers suggest God hears. God hears the cry of the oppressed and liberates them. It's a proclamation of faith about the nature of the liberating God, which is inspiring. For those who have felt it, such a proclamation endures and sustains.

Like all good rituals, it got all mixed up. Children danced. Women laughed. Men cried. The sacred ceremony captured their hearts and it morphed.

Baby Suggs spoke from her heart about what she knew to be true at that moment. She reminded each one that they were a gift and admonished each to love themselves with a fierce love.

Simplifying her words, she taught them a deep love. Love your hands. Love your mouth, love your eyes. Love your life-giving parts. Love your back. Love your neck. Touch those places, she suggested. And love them, now and always. This was the essence of her teaching.

Summarizing her teaching, she taught them about radical love in the face of hatred. Out there, they'd rather use your body to feed the pigs, rather use you for slop. They'd rather tie up your neck and your hands and your feet. Pay them no mind. You love your body and love all its perfect parts. Love them. Love them all. This was her teaching to her community.

This whole ritual, this whole sacred ceremony, was an act of radical resistance—to the slaveholder, to the slaveholders' religion and politics, to the culture at large that said these folks were less than human and unworthy.

Baby Suggs insisted that their very humanness was sacred and holy. Their bodies are sacred and holy.

She then gets to the thing to love above all else: your heart. She taught them that the heart was the prize and to love it above all else.

They walked back to their homes renewed, refreshed, transformed, and strengthened for all that was yet to come.

## PART 2 - THE UNCLES

The 1990s were a difficult decade for me. After college, I went to Washington, DC, to work for Senator Terry Sanford (D-NC). He was a giant to me. I felt like I had entered a dream when I got to be a part of his DC staff. In the summer of 1992, just before his re-election vote, he had open heart surgery. That November, he lost his re-election campaign. I was young and out of a job that I loved.

*There's nothing worse that can happen to me,* I thought.

The next month my father died. I realized that there was something harder than losing an election. I was in my mid-20s.

Throw in a tough breakup, and it was just an all-around rough time. Christmas of 1998, I decided I needed a vacation and I headed to my extended family in North Carolina. I picked up my cousin Derek and I drove him to Winston-Salem to his mom and dad's house, which annually hosted the Butts family Christmas. Derek and I went a bit earlier than normal and ended up stopping in China Grove. My uncle Archie, who spent his life as a small-town minister, was dying. Everyone knew this would be his last Christmas with us.

Tape recorder in hand, we went to see Archie. He was frail but spirited. He told stories about our grandfather, Vernie. Derek and I never met Vernie. None of our cousins did. He died well before any of us were born.

"He was the one who'd walk in the woods for hours, knew how to build whatever was needed, and told his eight children: Get an education. He was quiet, only talked when necessary," my uncle Archie said.

He told stories about my grandmother, Hazel. She was the tiniest adult you could imagine, but there was a resilience and a strength about her. She was the family's sun. Everything revolved around her. She died in 1985. Almost all his stories were about her.

Tears flew easily talking about her. As my grandfather was telling their children to get an education, my Grandmother Hazel was telling them to get Jesus. Derek and I grew up with her as a big presence. We knew her well.

Occasionally, out of the blue, amidst his storytelling, my Uncle Archie would start singing. He'd sing some old song my grandparents loved and sang to their children—my father, Derek's mother, and my aunts and uncles. They were old songs we had never heard before that day. It tickled him to sing those songs to us. "These are yours now," he said, "Keep them in your heart." One had something to do with being in a grove of peach trees and ending up with a lemon. He may have made that song up on the spot. We didn't care. It was perfect. We laughed. We sang. We danced. We cried. Like all good rituals, it morphed.

He blessed us with his old stories, laughter, and wisdom. This remembering helped us confront the reality of his coming death. It allowed us to think of the others who lived and died, who blessed the world in their living. His stories reminded us of our ancestors, now of blessed memory, but still somehow alive in his magical stories.

Christmas arrived. We gathered at Derek's parent's house. His mom, my dad's sister, is a big personality, sings operatic music, and has done so around the world. She has the biggest laugh imaginable, and a southern accent that makes everyone feel good—a genuine warmth. His dad is a minister, but not a small-town one. He's a famous one. And super warm and so attentive and wise.

Almost all my aunts and uncles were there. The food included barbecue and Cheerwine, authentic North Carolina food we all enjoyed growing up. During those growing-up days we'd gather at my grandmother's house—so many families, so many cousins, aunts, and uncles—for summer vacation and annual Christmas gatherings.

My uncle Gary knew that Derek and I had just experienced a powerful sacred ceremony of hearing the stories of a beloved uncle who was soon to die. He also knew we were both headed off to new projects. After a tough decade, I was headed to seminary in Washington, DC, to get my Master's in Divinity, an early step in the process of becoming a Unitarian Universalist minister.

Derek is a free spirit, with a master's degree in dance and a heart too big for seminary. He was about to go off to Austin to start a house church with an art space. He was going to teach homeless people how to dance away their pain and frustration. He was going to conduct outdoor worship services with prayer, music, and laughter.

We were both about to begin new lives with new adventures, both in the church of our upbringing and outside of it. I was a long way removed from my uncle Gary's Southern Baptist ministry as a budding Unitarian Universalist minister. Derek was deeply faithful, but his ministry was long removed from the traditional church building. We were both blazing new trails.

My uncle Gary wrote a book that has sold about a billion copies. At that point, he was not yet famous, and had not yet gone on Oprah. He was just Uncle Gary (and still is, to be honest). When he sends books to me and my beloved, he signs them: Above all, love.

At that moment, in Winston-Salem, North Carolina, with his son and his nephew, he took us to the kitchen, away from the family, with their laughter, eating, and stories.

He gave us a blessing. He prayed for us. He told us that he and the family could not be prouder of us.

We did not dance and laugh at that moment as we had with Uncle Archie. The laughter would come later when we tried to sing for everyone, The 12 Days of Christmas. We did not even cry.

We just received the blessing deep in our hearts, strengthened for the next thing and the next. Blessed beyond measure. Transformed.

In some small way, we were like those men, women, and children in the clearing. Uncle Archie remembered us. Uncle Gary reminded us to love ourselves so that we might love others.

And at that moment, the future came clear, grounded in relationship and community.

# THE CEREMONY

## PART 3: RITUALIZING RELATIONSHIP

Your relationship with your family has its own dynamics, its own rhythms, and stories. You may have biological aunts and uncles, grandparents, parents, or cousins you wish to memorialize and bless. You may have chosen family because your relationship with your biological family is fraught or non-existent. No matter what, you're invited to ritualize and bless your relationships.

A ritualizing relationship is an intentional creation of space that deepens the knowing of each other. We learn and know something new and deeper when we listen deeply to one another and our stories. In such rituals, we bless the past; we bless the present; we bless the future.

Some things you can do to create sacred space:

First, get clear about your own story. Write what is called an ethical will. This is a document that leaves a gift to your children and your children's children. Some can give financial estates that will provide for the needs of their descendants. Some can give them a house or a car. The ethical will is different. It is a profound gift that shares with your descendants the things you've learned, the values you wish to impart, and the stories you'd love to see endure.

Second, get a tape recorder (if you still have one of those ancient things) or a smartphone and sit with the loved ones in your life. Ask them some direct, simple, open-ended questions about their life, their loves, and their lessons. Ask them about your family and your family's family. Ask them about their guides, mentors, and teachers.

Third, remember to bless those around you—every chance you get. The president of Meadville Lombard Theological Seminary in Chicago says that every time he is on the phone with an elder family member, the first thing he does is ask for a blessing. My uncle Gary came to visit my family in Colorado Springs, years ago, when my children were very young. At the end of the visit, he looked at my child, Norah, then shy and reserved, peeking out behind a chair. "God has great things in store for you, Norah. Blessings." I'll never forget it. You too can bless those around you, whatever your spiritual, religious, or ethical framework.

Fourth, and this is huge, remember to love all of your parts, especially your heart. Every day, give some part of yourself a thank you. And then, dance, cry, laugh, for the living and the dead, and for those to come. In so doing, you bless your past, your present, and your future.

**Roger Butts** attended Wesley Theological Seminary in Washington, DC. He has been a Unitarian Universalist minister for 20 years. His writings have appeared in several anthologies. His first book, *Seeds of Devotion,* was published in 2021. Thanks to Kianna, the barista in Montgomery, Alabama, at the Troy University Bookstore and Café, who kept me caffeinated in the writing of this essay.

Connect with Roger:
Email: rogerbutts80905@gmail.com

CHAPTER 15

# WHO AM I REALLY?

## GATHERING THE FERTILE SOIL OF AUTHENTIC SELF

Rev. Shenna Lee-Belmore

## MY STORY

One day, at age 13, I was handed a bottle of Boones Farm Strawberry Hill wine. I immediately felt warm inside and could move beyond my ordinarily quiet, shy self. Of course, I now know that confidence wasn't real, yet at the time, it gave me some semblance of belonging and fitting in.

As a child, I never felt like I fit in or belonged anywhere —not with friends, schoolmates, or any groups I encountered. For most of my life, I envisioned myself standing behind a tree, peering at a world of people, places, and things I couldn't comprehend. Then, as I grew older, I realized I didn't belong in my family either, and I began to run away from home. At the core, I was desperately searching for something I could only find inside myself.

At about 11, I found some old papers showing I was adopted as a baby. Suddenly, my feeling that I didn't belong made sense.

*Who am I?*

It would be many years before I knew. Whenever the question arose, I drank. Drinking became my coping tool. I did unimaginable things to make sure I could continue to drink. It was the most effective method for drowning my sorrows and hopelessness and numbing my feelings. Running away was another coping mechanism. I always felt like if I could get far enough away from where I was, I'd somehow be able to find my true self.

I remained lost in alcoholism for 17 years. I don't remember a lot of it. When it finally got bad enough, at the age of 30, I got sober. It was a difficult journey, and, along the way, I often found myself waking up in an adult world with only the mental and emotional maturity of a 13-year-old to rely on. When I picked up alcohol at that young age, it was like I stopped growing on every level.

Without alcohol, and with nowhere left to run, I had to find new ways to cope with my feelings of isolation. I began taking various classes and courses and acquired many certifications, all in an attempt to prove I was somebody. No matter how much I achieved, I was never satisfied and found myself continually searching.

I married at 16, divorced at 21; married at 28; divorced again at 29; married at 30, divorced yet again at 31; married at 33, and divorced at 34. Ironically, all those name changes resulted in furthering my confusion about who I was. I even went to court at age 35 to petition to get my birth name back. My adoptive parents named me Debra Lee Ganger, but I knew my birth name was Shenna. It was on the adoption papers. And Shenna is the name I chose. Perhaps it would help me to get to know myself. I didn't want my adopted family's last name, nor any of my former husbands' names, so I kept my adoptive middle name—Lee—and it became my last name.

*Who am I?* The question screamed louder as I looked at my portfolio of accomplishments with various last names on the certificates. Even my birth name felt foreign.

*Who am I?*

I experienced the first inklings of peace about my identity when I arrived and began attending Native American gatherings and ceremonies. *This feels like home. I love everything about these people and these ways!* After a time it became apparent that I needed to find a teacher and dig deeper.

My first elder and mentor was Comanche and Blackfoot. She taught me her style of women's traditional dance. When I learned enough, I was thrilled to dance in the sacred circle at pow-wows, even becoming Head Lady Dancer at many of them through the years.

Fourteen years later, a new elder came into my life. She was of northeast woodland heritage; Lenape', Oneida, and Santee. From her, I learned the northern style of women's traditional dance. Amazingly, after all the years of dancing southern, I immediately embraced these new steps. It all flowed. *Is this my true heritage?*

Through the years, so much kept pointing to the Shawnee people. There were hints from others that my birth father, whom I never met or knew, was a half-breed Shawnee, and I was born in a part of Ohio the Shawnee had inhabited in the distant past. *Are these people part of my heritage?*

I took a DNA test and anxiously awaited the results. When they arrived, I felt crushed. The results showed only traces of Native DNA. The percentages were scattered all over: Ireland, Scotland, Wales, Great Britain, and on and on. I'd met my birth mother when I was 11 and was told she had some Gaelic ancestry, but where were the Native parts? *Have I been living a lie all these years, inauthentically playing at being Native American? I've been living that path, embodying it, and feel led to it—now what?*

I had no idea what to do next so I took my pain to my elder. After some consideration, she suggested I journey to where I was born, Ohio. She gave me a task that would change my life, a simple and meaningful ceremony. "Gather soil from your homeland and bring it back. In this way, you'll carry home with you."

I recognize this sounds like an easy thing to do, but I lived in Florida at the time, so this meant taking time off work and figuring out how I'd get there. "Wouldn't it be better to simply ask a friend in Ohio to send some soil," I asked her. "No. Shortcuts aren't the answer. You must make the entire journey on your own," I was told.

I began to gather items I felt called to have with me: my drum, a rattle, my bundle of sacred herbs, my pipe, a smudge bowl, matches, a special container for collecting the soil, necessities like food, drinking water, and clothing. I made a bed in the back of my Jeep in case I got tired on the road and made sure there was money in the bank. Once all of that was done, I headed out.

I prayed a lot along the way, stopping at places that called to me, resting in roadside rest stops as needed, until I finally reached my destination,

Piqua, Ohio, the town in which I was born. I checked into a motel at the edge of town, settled in, and made a plan. This trip wasn't about connecting with old friends, nor my adopted family; this trip was fully about finding and connecting with myself.

During my teenage years of running away, there were a handful of places I always hid and often drank. Ironically, these were the places that called to me when it was time to collect soil. First stop; a park close by, one that used to house the town's public swimming pool. It was filled with trees and nature and had a lovely creek running through it. Fetching items from the Jeep, I assembled them on a blanket by the stream and offered smudge to the four directions: to the above realms, below realms, all my relations, and to the Creator. I drummed and prayed, "Grandmothers and grandfathers of the four winds and the in-betweens, loving ancestors, family, and friends I come to you in a good way, giving thanks for this time and journey, thanking you in advance for clarity in this long search for self. Thank you for this bit of earth from my homeland. I am blessed by it, and so it is."

I gently loosened some earth from this spot and placed it in a special glass jar, then gave thanks for this place and for the memories. When this act was complete, I packed up, and headed for my next stop.

I felt called to the Great Miami River. That side of town was referred to as Shawnee. I lived in that area for many years and often walked the levee bank to sit and look at the waters. With my sacred items in hand, I walked to the water's edge, laying out my drum, smudge bowl, and glass jar. Once more, I prayed, stating my desires, then I sat quietly for a while in reflection. I drummed and sang to the ancestors, then gathered a bit more soil to add to the jar.

Again, I packed up and drove to another location. This time, I gathered my items and walked into the woods. I stopped by another stream, which eventually connected with the river, and set up my altar. I prepared the herbs in the smudge bowl, prayed, then sat in reflection on the years past, when I sat in this very spot. I was awestruck when it occurred to me that, all these many years later, I was here again, asking the same question I'd asked then! This time, however, a new question arose: *Am I really ready to know my truth? Yes,* I heard myself answer unequivocally. *I am present and open to receiving.*

Before arriving, I knew I was to visit four places to gather my soil. I packed everything up and headed to the fourth and final spot, an ancient cemetery adjacent to the old Johnston Farm. *I wonder why I always feel such a pull and connection to this place. I find such peace here.*

The cemetery is filled with old tombstones and monuments dating back as far as 1812, making it the oldest cemetery in the area. Interestingly, I discovered later that it's believed Colonel Johnston's brother was the first person buried in this cemetery. His body was brought back from Indiana by a Shawnee Indian named Logan.

There was a huge cedar tree off to one side of the cemetery in the same clearing I went to when I ran away from home as a child. I'd wander through the graves and sit under that tree. It seemed to be the last of the four places I was to gather earth.

Using the same process, I set up my altar under the old cedar tree. I smudged all around, sang, drummed, and prayed. Tears began to flow as I thought of the past and pondered the intent of this journey. *I'm actually here, doing all this!* I gathered a bit of earth, added it to the jar, and gave thanks through my tears. As I turned the lid to seal the jar, I knew the ceremony was complete.

In all the years I lived there, 25 to be exact, I never actually visited the Johnston Farm to take the tour and this seemed a perfect time. The tour guide offered a thorough account of those times. "Colonel Johnston was the Indian agent for the government when the war of 1812 broke out. He was literally the Indian agent for the Shawnee! In fact, over sixteen hundred Shawnees were allowed to stay on this very land in order to be safe during the war. The agency continued until 1829. Even after the war, Native Americans continued to arrive here seeking aid. Colonel Johnston had become a trusted friend."

I was surprised and a bit shocked. It was all coming together and making sense. I realized the Shawnee lived on the grounds I'd visited so many times as a child, and many had died and were buried here in unmarked graves. I'd been with them in some of the most difficult moments of my life.

We wrapped up the tour with a canal boat ride. Drawn by a mule, we were shown how transportation and trading happened back then. The canal is now blocked off at a certain point and no longer open to the Great Miami River, but the Shawnee traveled those waters, camped, and lived along its banks. All those places I ran away to those many years ago, when I needed to drown my sorrows, were all places the Shawnee lived, traded, and died.

As amazing as that all is, doubt still crept in occasionally. *What about the DNA test results?* The question is no longer useful. I've learned a vast majority of Native Americans refuse to have their DNA tests taken; thus, there aren't major stores to pull data from. Perhaps this will change with time and I will test again. For now, no matter what the test says about my DNA, this journey was, by far, one of the most important events of my life. It allowed me to trust what I know intuitively. Through my elder, Spirit orchestrated this journey to show me there's a genuine connection somehow. In the years since then, I've practiced what my elders taught me to the best of my ability. These teachings are real and as familiar as my own hand. Visiting these sites and doing this ceremony changed me over time and helped me to find the place where I belong.

I've said for years, "What you see is what you get with me." I've learned to be authentically myself. No document, DNA test, nor certification of any sort is who I am. Instead, I'm a beautiful combination of an ancestral lineage that's multicultural. I have a basket full of beauty to pull from, and I love who I've become.

If you've arrived at the end of my sharing, my wish is that it inspires you and assists you in creating your own journey to your true self. Here are a few instructions to guide you.

## THE CEREMONY

If possible, return to your homeland. If this isn't possible, remember we're all born of this Earth. Anywhere you are, at any given moment, is connected to all the places you've previously been. The intention is everything, so find a place that feels sacred and right for you.

Gather items like drinking water, a vessel for soil, a drum, a rattle or chime, a smudge bowl, and herbs. These can be found at most metaphysical stores. Smudge is used for purifying your surroundings, yourself, and as an offering to Spirit. Incense can work as well. Light your incense or herbs, pray and send smoke to each direction. To the east: sweetgrass, honoring spring, the element of air and new beginnings. To the west: sage, honoring fall, the element of water, time of evening, and slowing down. To the north: tobacco, honoring winter, the element of earth, the time of full night, and complete rest. To the south: cedar, honoring summer, the element of fire, the time of midday, life, and love.

Honoring the directions in this order traditionally opens a path of new beginnings. Honor each direction, as explained, for balance and clarity in your quest. Speak your desires and intentions to Spirit, asking for a deeper understanding of who you truly are. Pray in your own way and in your own words. Here's an example, in case those words are hard to find: "Beloved Spirit, Creator, Mother, Father God, I come to you in a good way, seeking clarity for my path and understanding of my authentic self. I offer these herbs, prayers, and music to you as a gift. Thank You."

Drum, rattle, sing, then be still and listen. Answers may float in softly over time or come suddenly. Drink water, and share some with the earth where you sit. Gather a small amount of soil and place it in your vessel. Give thanks once again for this journey. Take the soil home and allow it to bring the energy of your true self into your awareness.

**Shenna Lee-Belmore** is the owner and operator of Mountain Healing Center. She lives to inspire others, facilitating healing on all levels—body, mind, and spirit.

Shenna began her own healing journey by learning Usui Reiku in 1989 and became a practitioner/teacher by 1994. She's studied Pranic Healing, is certified in Emotional Soma Relationships, and is a reflexologist. Shenna became an ordained Interfaith Minister several years ago, as a step along her path toward assisting others.

Shenna utilizes her empathic abilities, as well as personal experience to walk others to the door of health. Her passion lies in assisting others through and past the trauma that holds them back from being all they can; as others helped her along the way.

Shenna can be found on Facebook at Mountain Healing Center or https://mountainhealingcenter.weebly.com

# CHAPTER 16

# THE UNSEEN TRUTH

## A JOURNEY TO DISCOVERING YOUR TRUE ROOTS AND SELF WORTH

Milagros Ruiz Bello, Curandera, Musical Healer, Theta Healer®

## MY STORY

*Who am I? Why do I feel this? What am I seeing?!*

My very first ceremony.

I recall not wanting to do this. I feared losing control. Something told me to go through with it. I felt my grandmothers with me. Mother Earth coursed through me. The unconditional love that most describe when connecting to Source.

Here's what brought me to this point.

**I lost my voice.**

My depression was so great not even music filled my heart. With all I was going through, I didn't feel any music in me. I felt so belittled. My partner was so mean. I felt no support coming from him. There are times I can still hear his criticism. "It was pretty good," he speaks with disdain, or "I don't think you can do that song." It took a lot for me to open up again.

Parts of my voice were taken over the course of years of mental and physical abuse that very few witnessed. There were times I hid behind my joy and other times I hid behind love songs. These were ways I tried to be open without expressing myself directly to others. But this time it was different. I didn't want to sing at all.

I was molested by a family member at the tender age of five, raped at 14, and in many abusive relationships thereafter. It was as if I couldn't get out of the hole I didn't see existed.

*Why in the hell does shit keep happening to me?* This was always the internal argument. *I don't harm anyone. I'm a caring person. I don't take more than what I need and yet, I always get shit thrown at me! Why?!*

This is the mental debate most of us go through when we're hit with difficult challenges, whether we're born into a "good" family or not. I've seen it all. The lower frequencies of abuse and despair don't discriminate. They don't care if you're black, white, or brown, nor do they care where your ancestors came from, or who they were. What matters is you recognize the patterns (when the frequencies are low) and do something to change this—raise your vibration.

Accepting the lessons is also key. What are we to learn from these challenges? Self-worth? The discovery of your true roots? Or both?

Plant medicine helped me see the unseen truth of how all my generational traumas were affecting me in the now. Plant medicine worked for me. But let's face it, many have been brainwashed to think that all plant medicines are bad for you, and therefore we should fear them. Not only that, but governments have rightly made most of them illegal because many of us have abused the use of them. Most of us weren't taught to respect them rather than fear them.

The truth is, scientists all over the world are trying to understand how plant medicines work and the benefits they can bring to people. However, these experts are missing the key. Their key element is unseen and not a tangible thing. You can't touch a spirit in this 3D world. You can't touch the soul or an angel; therefore, in most cases, such is not believed to exist.

Sacred ceremonies originate from our ancestors.

The elders hold sacred ceremonies all over the world—spiritual rituals shunned by many organized religions. Do we, healers, believe in a God? Yes. Yes, we do! We believe in the Divine Source so much that we defend the waters of this Earth, the trees, and the animals. We're called tree huggers as if this is an offensive term for us.

Sacred ceremonies don't always include plant medicines. Some people can tap into their higher self with a simple meditation practice.

## MY FIRST JOURNEY WITH LOS NIÑOS SANTOS (THE SACRED CHILDREN)

An awakening.

I lit the sage to cleanse the space. (An indigenous ritual to clear out any negative energies.) As the fire burned the leaves, I motioned with my hands, as if the smoke could be gathered as one would gather water from a flowing river, collecting the smoke and showering my being with it. I closed my eyes and prayed silently, *Great Mother, protect me and my sacred space from any and all unwelcomed entities. May only those who come from love and light enter this space.* As I took another breath I also called upon my grandmothers. *Grandmothers, Rosa and Carmelita, please be with me tonight. Guide me through this journey. Allow me to feel your presence and love.*

I picked up the abalone shell where I had placed the lit sage and walked to the forward berth, the bedroom of the boat. *Great spirit, Anastasia; Jesus, please protect me and this space.* Making sure all corners of the room were smudged, I turned to the head (restroom), opened the door, and smudged all four corners as well. I then continued to the salon (living room) and galley (kitchen). "No entity is allowed in my sacred space. May I be protected from anything not meant to be here," I whispered. Once the smudging below deck was complete, I proceeded to the outside of the boat, smudging all around the classic 38 Downeaster sailboat.

The Pacific Ocean is one of the biggest portals on Earth; therefore, a thorough cleanse is needed before any ceremony.

After a couple of hours, I saw something. It wasn't pleasant. In fact, for a split second, it freaked me out, because what I was seeing was a dark entity! It looked like an older man. It looked at me, taunting me, "I am here." Then the courage of my great-grandmother took over and I did a limpia (a cleanse or energy clearing) to rid the space of this unwanted being. As I cleansed the space it was invading, my breathing changed. It was as if I was sucking this being out, spitting him off and out of the boat where the ceremony was taking place.

Once the space was cleared below deck, I looked up at what was supposed to be the white lining of the ceiling of the boat, but instead I saw black space. As if the ceiling wasn't there at all. I saw Aztec patterns that were constantly changing. I was having beautiful visions. All this came to me in black and white. I felt no fear. I tried to focus on the messages, but it was nearly impossible. I even tried to look beyond the patterns, but that, too, seemed an impossible task.

My whole body felt as if it was being charged. The waves of energy reaching me were subtle. The energies perceived that night are still unexplainable. I can not put words to most of what happened. All I can tell you is that I began to visualize who I truly am. My calling to follow in the footsteps of my ancestors. My true roots. My indigenous roots. And, as I move forward, I continue to work to integrate what I felt and saw.

Over a year later, I found out that one of my great-aunts still had my great-grandmother's books—the teachings of the Aztecs in medicinal herbs. I cried with joy. The first thought I had was, *I must go visit her and scan these books!* I was always drawn to learning more about herbs and her books were a great tool to have since they remained in the family for so many years! And now I have found them!

The information that came to me during my first ceremony started making sense over a period of time. My only regret was not asking my great-grandmother more questions on curanderismo (healing) when she was still alive. She lived to be 103!

## SITTING WITH GRANDMOTHER AYA. (AYAHUASCA)

During an ayahuasca ceremony, both grandmothers came to me and offered their love and guidance. It was a peaceful journey. They came to sit and teach me how to just be. "Be still," they said. "Trust the process. You don't always have to know it all." My response, in thought, was, *I just don't want to make anymore mistakes.* "It's the mistakes that take us where we need to go and show us what we need to let go of," Grandma Rosa replied. As she said this I saw all the pain she held on to, all the resentment and bitterness. She's an example of what not to do. **Holding on to pain will keep us trapped in our own pain.**

Both my great-grandmother on my mother's side and grandmother on my father's side come to visit when I'm doing any type of ceremony. They're the ones who guide me through the process. They're the reason I've built so much trust in my intuition.

I've had several ceremony experiences and each was different. Some were more intense than others.

In one case, I lay there in a dark candle-lit room, not being able to really move, and my soul left my body. Hard to explain how, but I simply knew I was floating into nothingness. It was a dark but peaceful place where I knew nothing mattered. It wasn't scary, as many associate darkness with evil. It was the most beautiful peace I've ever felt.

One is able to "journey" without the assistance of plant medicines, but most are fearful of doing so, as sometimes one can forget to breathe and have some fear of getting lost in the nothingness. I recall pausing and thinking, *I have to go back and breathe,* and just by having such a thought, I was back in my body. I took a breath, and out I went again, into that nothingness.

Think of it this way. If you've ever had a dream where you found yourself looking at yourself sleeping, that's exactly what it feels like.

Plant medicine and other holistic healing modalities have been a part of this world for thousands of years, even before Jesus walked the Earth, yet there are those who call these sacred rituals "new age" or evil. It has been very difficult for me to accept that people think in this way because I know the Creator. The love that exists in the nothingness space I speak of is an amazing one—one that is beautiful and beyond our understanding.

Plant medicine isn't just about the plants that allow us to see things we otherwise can't see. Plant medicine is many common-day things: having hot tea right before bed, using sage or copal to clear out your sacred space, and spending time in nature.

When using plant medicines, go back to your true roots. Try to find where your family came from. Go as far back as you possibly can. In doing so, you'll find so many answers to questions such as: "Why do I feel so sad all the time?" or "Why am I a cheater?" or "Why do I criticize everyone?" We all carry baggage from generations ago. These patterns didn't start with you. You carry memories in your DNA. But what will you do about it? Can you heal generational trauma?

Healing doesn't happen overnight. For some of us it has taken years. For others, decades. The important thing is you acknowledge the patterns, accept the lessons, and learn from what you're shown and told. Do your shadow work (explore your darker impulses). Integrate (work with the lessons given to you!). So many healers can give you a hand when you fall into a hole, but only you can pull yourself up. They can't do the work for you, but they can help you understand what you're feeling.

Remember, it doesn't matter how many times you try; the important thing is that you don't ever give up. Every time you try, you heal a part of yourself and your lineage. You heal not only yourself but generations to come.

There are several rituals one can complete to connect back with your true self. With these you'll also learn to recognize your self-worth. I'm truly grateful for what I've learned and continue to discover. I'm grateful for the lessons and the teachers of both the good and bad.

My hope is that you, too, will find your way, not only into healing, but discovering who you truly are.

# THE CEREMONY

Cleansing and protecting your space (also known as smudging).

This ritual can be done in one room, an entire house, your car, or any other personal spaces.

Any of these tools or herbs can be used depending on what's available to you:

- Copal
- Sage
- Rosemary
- Dragons Blood
- Palo santo

Extra tool: Feather (for smudging)

You can also use crystals for added protection, but they are not necessary. These are just some of the crystals recommended for protection:

- Clear Quartz
- Amethyst
- Black Obsidian

- Black Tourmaline
- Pyrite

Safe containers for burning herbs:

- Copalero (which are usually found in Latin American markets or mystic shops)
- Ceramic bowl
- Abalone shell
- Small cauldron
- Granite bowl and sand

One can also carry a "medicine bag" with some crystals and other sacred items. A medicine bag (for those who aren't familiar) is a small pouch that is either made of leather, woven, or crocheted. This is often small enough to carry around your neck and under your shirt, in your pants pocket, and some women carry it in their purse.

I strongly advise you to follow your intuition when choosing your tools. Once you've gathered your tools, please do the ceremony in a safe manner, as you'll be working with fire.

Be sure to have a journal or an audio recorder handy in case you receive messages (also known as downloads).

**Step 1:** As you stand over your tools, close your eyes. Imagine a light that comes in from above, in through your head. Simultaneously, you also receive light from the depths of the Earth, through the souls of your feet. This light travels through your body and meets in the center, illuminating your being with love and light. You will not necessarily see this light, but you may feel it.

Take three deep breaths, in through your nose and out of your mouth, while you envision pure love within.

Now open your eyes, and give a small bow in gratitude to self and Source while placing your hands over your heart.

**Step 2:** Light your sacred tool and place it in a fire-safe container of your choice. Once it's lit, walk around your space and be sure the smoke is smudged using a feather or your hand, into every corner of the room(s). Also, open closets to allow the smoke to cleanse that space and don't forget to smudge all the mirrors as well.

As you smudge, you can speak or ask the "bad" to leave and your space to be protected. If you prefer to pray, you may do so. If you don't know what to say, please see the paragraph below. You may create your own saying or prayer once you get more comfortable with smudging.

*May You, Divine Source, Creator, be with me as I cleanse my sacred space. May my angels or guides assist me in protecting my space and may my ancestors be with me. To all those who work with love and light, may you illuminate my being and allow for any negativity to exit. May all my guardians keep me and my space free of any despair. May all darkness transmute into love and light. I ask this pure of heart and trust that Source is with me always. A'ho.*

This can be repeated throughout all the rooms or any new spaces you encounter. You can also add or modify it to honor your beliefs.

**Step 3:** Place crystals near areas of concern. If you're having trouble sleeping, I suggest placing an amethyst on your nightstand or under your pillow. This can be done before or after smudging.

You can also carry your crystals in your medicine bag while you smudge your space.

◊ **If you are clearing your space in preparation for a ceremony or meditation, please continue to the next steps.**

**Step 4:** Sit or lay comfortably with your crystal or medicine (tea or otherwise). Bring your intention forward (this is also referred to as setting intentions) and receive the messages meant for you, if any. Allow all feelings to come to you. Remember, in order to heal, you must feel. If you need to laugh, then laugh. If you need to cry, then cry. It's a form of releasing and letting go of things that no longer serve your higher purpose.

**Step 5:** Make time for integration! This is very important. If doing medicine, please allow yourself at least a couple of days to have some peace and journal anything that comes to mind. If you have a session with a healer, keep a journal handy. There will be times when you may receive downloads (also known as messages) in the form of random thoughts. Honor your space and time to process these. Even if what you write down doesn't make sense, at some point it might, so write it down!

**Step 6:** Slowly come back into your real-time space by wiggling your fingers and toes; open your eyes, and sit up. Give thanks to Source and any other angels or spirits that assisted during your journey.

Also, be very mindful of what you feed your being. Try your best not to watch anything (movies or television) that will stir negative feelings. If doing plant medicines, follow the "dieta" (diet) recommended.

Be kind and patient with yourself. Healing takes time and there is no miracle "medicine" that will magically take all your traumas, addictions, or pain away. Healing, and learning healing methods, is a lifelong journey in this 3D world.

May love and light accompany you throughout your sacred journey.

Intuitive healer **Milagros Ruiz Bello Martinez Arambula** comes from a lineage of healers. Her gifts started surfacing at the age of five and later, her visionary abilities returned when she made the decision to answer the call. Some consider her to be a jack of all trades. She chooses to use this designation to her advantage.

A love of music has always played a huge role in her life with over 25 years of experience. She often creates healing music during her meditations and curative ceremonies. As she puts it, "Mother Earth takes over and guides my voice and drum."

Overall, Milagros considers herself to be a perpetual student. Her great grandmother practiced the ways of the Aztecs, and although her ancestor leaves big shoes to fill, Milagros is taking on the challenge wherever it may lead her.

In her spare time she likes to create medicine bags and other crocheted items. She enjoys making custom drums and other ceremonial pieces as much as creating music. She connects with Pachamama by spending time in nature.

Her mission is to help people remember their true roots as she continues to learn about her own. She aspires to become increasingly educated about different cultures and healing modalities in order to better understand and relate to all the inhabitants of this planet.

"I am you, you are me, we are one."

# SERVICES

**Healing modalities offered:**

– Energetic clearings

– Oracle readings

– Shamanic works

– Sound & drum healing

– Meditations & Ceremonies

**Other services:**

– Gift discovery

– Spiritual, integration, self-love guidance

– Shadow work

– Translations (English and Spanish)

– Bilingual voice-overs

Connect with Milagros:

To connect and learn more about Milagros and her self-discovery, healing journey, and more services:

Website: www.milagrosmbs.com

Instagram: @conamormilagros @miss_milly_jay

Facebook Page: Con Amor, Milagros

Email: milagrosruizbello@gmail.com

# CHAPTER 17

# HEAL YOUR SPIRITUAL WOUNDS

## THE RITES OF MARY MAGDALENE

Maeven Eller-Five,
Community Organizer, Spiritual Guide, Psychic Tarot Reader

The path that led me to the mysteries of Mary Magdalene was a difficult one fraught with willful intentions to cast me as someone unworthy of God's salvation. Such inequities ultimately set my foot on the path to a greater understanding of the Magdalene and the Feminine Divine.

## MY STORY

I still remember it like it was yesterday. It was 4th grade, and there I was, so proudly dressed in my Girl Scout uniform, sash, hat, and gloves. I worked very hard to earn those badges. For the first time, I attended the Sunday morning service at St. Louis Catholic Church. Being one of the few non-Catholics in my troop, I was excitedly looking forward to this day. My heart was pounding in my chest.

As we reached the inner doors of the sanctuary, I could hear the organ music playing. The opulence I always dreamed of became visible just inside. I began to tremble. The line moved forward and tears were hot in my eyes.

When the time came for communion, like every other scout before me, I rose from our appointed pew. I followed along making my way to the front of the church, where I knelt in front of the altar.

The Priest, so finely dressed in his robes, slowly made his way down the row sharing the blood and body of Christ with all who knelt before him. As he came to stand before me, he was flanked by two altar boys holding the wafers and the cup. The Priest's eyes fell upon me. I smiled, hands folded. He paused for a moment as if something was wrong. I could see him realize he didn't recognize me. Then, in front of the entire church, he looked at me as if I was something unfit, something unholy. I began to shrink under his condemning stare, then something inside me grew stronger and I found a strength unbeknownst to me before. The Priest denied me communion and with eyes that clearly condemned me for my transgression, he abruptly motioned for me to return to our pew all alone.

Moments before, I'd been seeking God. Now I found myself denied by His servant who sent me away. I felt my face flush as I rose to return to the pew, but something warm enveloped me, building a small fire inside me. As I turned to face the congregation, I could see eyes hardened against me, revealing me as an interloper, one not worthy of any part of their Christ. In fiery defiance, I didn't bow my head in the shame they sought of me. Instead I held my head high as I returned to my seat.

"It wasn't just that you aren't Catholic," my Girl Scout Leader told me the next day. "Somehow they knew you were born out of wedlock." My mother was being shamed for something neither of us had any choice in. Being from a small town, it didn't take long for me to find out that my biological father was in the congregation that day. I hear his communion was unimpeded by the aforementioned disruptive events of the day. Good for him.

That day, at the St. Louis Catholic Church, was the first of many occurrences in my life. I was often turned away for the circumstances of my birth. Still, despite the obstacles put before me on my spiritual path, I continued reaching out to God. Imagine my pleasure when the Magdalene claimed me, wrapping me in the nurturing arms of the Divine Feminine.

Over the next several decades, I encountered many forms and faces of the Divine Feminine—but the Magdalene is where my heart found its home.

Quite often, women felt marginalized within the traditional church. They frequently seek elsewhere for something that spiritually resonates with them, deep in their souls. Such has been my journey. I found myself in the welcoming embrace of the goddess. Like the ancestors before me, the goddess guided me to tribal roots, opening the way for a life of service.

I founded an organization called Betwixt & Between Community Center. It was part of our mission statement to create a safe place to share the joys of an accepting and welcoming community with other like minds. It was there, within those programs and sacred walls, The Goddess Box was born, providing a safe place for women to commune with the goddess in all her facets.

"I want all women to understand the power of our sacred femininity," I told the women who found their way to the community. "The Goddess lurks in the sway of our hips at a drum circle around the revel fire. Our sensuality is a part of her essence. The lessons of The Magdalene are about all the sides of our her-story. It's part of the DNA that flows in our bloodlines."

In The Goddess Box, we discussed how to worship the Divine Feminine. We sought her wherever she revealed herself to us. We opened our eyes to all the ways she was reflected within society, like a beacon, and also came to recognize how often the feminine was treated as something to be shamed. While she could be found throughout ancient cultures, in their myths, and in Gnosticism, she has been more recently brought to the forefront of our imaginations by the resurgence of earth-based religions, eco-spirituality, and the Neo-Pagan movement. Today, the goddess can be found in the growing metaphysical and new-age community, and faith-based topics and workshops are more accessible.

It's important to note that The Goddess Box was significant in inspiring us to lift ourselves up by releasing our own limiting thoughts. Growth doesn't happen unless you turn the soil once in a while. *You have to step into the murky waters of self-doubt and loathing,* I considered. *You must have the courage to wade out into the deep end to process your own self-defeating behaviors.* It can be absolutely terrifying and completely liberating. Admitting to these limiting ideas, birthed by our shadow selves and old wounds, opens us to a powerful practice of personal responsibility. As a group, we embraced our union like shield maidens of old, each and every one of us bravely going into a self-care battle.

As happened, our group, as a whole, seemed to be experiencing a great deal of negativity in their lives. The common crime was demanding spiritual self-governance. Ah, the audacity of us all.

Angela showed up one afternoon to plan our upcoming Goddess Box Circle. She was obviously upset and had once again been marginalized by her family because of her spiritual pursuits. She was not alone in her frustrations. Many of us had been similarly categorized by those we loved.

As directors of a spiritual non-profit, both of us frequently heard from women who found themselves the victims of mistreatment or civil rights transgressions. This often happened to women who expressed an interest in earth-based spirituality, new age topics, or their own indigenous faiths. Our sisters in The Goddess Box were targeted at work, and even fired for things as simple as having a crystal or candle on their desks. Times are a bit better now, but then, mothers regularly found themselves in court fighting for their parental rights after being accused of practicing witchcraft or devil worship by their partners or family members.

So here, at this moment, Angela sat before me, with that hard look she often gets in her eyes when she makes her mind up. It was clear Mary Magdalene was the perfect choice for our circle gathering. Something sacred began to bloom between us, as it so often did. In this moment of hurt and strength, The Rites of Mary Magdalene was born.

We sent out our full moon circle invites right on time. In the special instructions, we made certain to emphasize attendees were going to be asked to take their shoes off and would be barefoot during the ceremony. We chose to reveal no other details. I still believe this is an extremely important part of the impact of this ceremony. As I look back, I am reminded how sometimes it's easiest to bare your soul once your feet are free and unhindered. At least, that's how it was for us that magical night, all those moons ago.

A great deal of the work I do today is born out of the desire to help seekers find their way past any unwanted spiritual bondage. My work helps others to release misguided guilt and shame. That was the work of this particular circle of women and I still feel the ripples of profound healing we experienced. Most of all, I remember taking a knee at the altar beside Angela with the desire to invoke a moment with Feminine Divine. Unlike all those years ago in my Girl Scout uniform, the Magdalene did not turn us away. She cleansed our hearts of hurt, and filled them with love.

That night, we offered one of the most moving experiences I have ever facilitated. We were completely unprepared for the humbling response the women in The Goddess Box had as Angela and I knelt before them to wash their feet. Floodgates opened and feelings of unworthiness and pain poured forth in tears. Pain transmuted to pleasure as, one by one, each woman recognized herself as holy and worthy. The beauty of this memory remains a healing one for me, personally, and I hear its the same for other attendees all these years later.

# THE CEREMONY

Mary Magdalene is known to many of us as Christ's companion, his most favored. She has often been called a repentant whore, or a fallen woman in more traditional religions. Perhaps most remembered for being the one Jesus let wash his feet with her tears—the Magdalene's story is ever-changing. She has come to represent the Feminine Divine and connects women with many goddesses, offering them her wild, unrestrained strength. She is a symbol of forgiveness, firm commitment to loved ones, strength, and vulnerable love.

To begin any sacred act, the most important thing is to set your intentions. Still yourself. Hold in your mind your desired results. In this rite, focused thought is placed in helping your attendees shed themselves of any limiting ideas about their sacred relationship with the Holy. Doing so empowers their spiritual journey moving forward.

## CREATING YOUR SACRED SPACE

1. Clean the space and make it ready to receive your attendees.

2. Lay out your circle. You will need an appropriately sized table for an altar in the center of your ritual area. It will hold your tools and ritual items. You may make your altar setting for your sacred space as elaborate or as simple as you feel called to do. In this ceremony you'll also want to have chairs set in a circle, one for each participant.

Make sure there is an entrance into the space. I recommend you set this entrance in the west, as the west is the direction often associated with the element associated with water.

3. You'll need a basin to hold water. It could be a dish pan. You'll also need a pitcher of warm water and a cup of rose petals (or more if many people are joining you). Prepare a towel for each participant, or, for ease, you may ask those coming to bring one along.

4. On the altar set a candle and matches. You'll light this candle as you welcome the essence of Mary Magdalene into your space through prayer or words of acknowledgment.

5. A chalice of spring water or wine, and a plate of cakes or cookies can also be included and will help your guests ground after the ceremony.

When you begin, hold in your mind what you hope to accomplish. The intention of this rite is to help your attendees release all shame, guilt, or feelings of alienation from God. In this ceremony, it's your aim to guide each member of your rite to connect to the Feminine Divine in a meaningful way. Hold in your heart the potential for each person to move past any feelings of spiritual inadequacy.

*"We all come from the goddess and to her we shall return, like a drop of rain, flowing to the ocean."*

A chant sung by many. Author unknown.

Once all of your guests have arrived and removed their shoes, invite them to line up to come into the circle. Have them bring their towels with them.

Greet your guests with a welcoming blessing as they enter and ask each attendee to move around the circle in the order they entered.

Explain in your own words why you've brought them together to share in this moment of healing and spiritual cleansing, then ask everyone to place their towel in the chair behind them and remain standing. Step into the opening in the west where they entered to join in the circle. Have your guests join hands. Instruct everyone to take in a cleansing breath.

"Breath in the potential healing available to you and exhale that which no longer serves you." Once everyone is settled by breath, seal the circle. Ask each person to pass a hand squeeze to the person on their left. You initiate the action and the hand squeeze passes from person to person around the circle. When the squeeze comes back to your right hand, state, "This circle is cast. So mote it be." Everyone may sit now.

Take a moment to walk the circle in a clockwise direction and speak from your heart about why you're hosting this circle. Share your intentions to help them find spiritual healing and a greater connection to the Feminine Divine in all her many aspects.

Take your place at the altar.

Welcome the energy of Mary Magdalene into the circle. Speak from your heart. When you've invoked her energy, light the candle at the center of your altar. Then add rose petals to the basin of your choice. Roses are a symbol of The Magdalene and her work. Pour the warm water on top of them. Use your right hand to blend the water and the petals.

"Who among you has a memory of being made to feel less as a woman, a second-class spiritual being, by organized religion or society?" Ask them to consider what they would like to share about that. Start by sharing your own story, then let the group organically discuss their experiences, allowing enough time for all to speak. Be prepared for their pain and hurt to emerge.

When all have finished speaking their truth, it is time to introduce a chant. I often use this one:

*"Strong like the waterfall. Gentle like the rain.*
*River wash my tears away, Astarte. (Ah - Star- te)."*

Attribution unknown.

As the chant begins, take your basin to the first chair to the left, past the western entrance. Ask for the attendee's towel. Place the towel under their feet. Reach into the water and take some of the rose petals in your hands and begin to use them to gently wash their feet.

Make your way around the circle repeating the process. Be prepared for the emotional response you may encounter. Angela and I were taken aback by the way our dear sisters of The Goddess Box felt unworthy to have their feet washed; the way they melted into feeling worthy, sacred, and a part of the Divine, still moves me to tears.

There, on my knees in front of my sisters, and beside Angela in all her strength, I found the part of God I had been looking for all those years ago, the Divine Feminine, and it was good.

**Maeven Eller-Five** is the owner of Maeven's Magickal Life, where she is a community organizer and ritualist, a noted psychic and tarot reader, an event and festival coordinator, and a spiritual guidepost for her clients and students. She's a workshop coordinator on various topics relating to spiritual growth and development and writes articles on related topics.

Maeven has devoted her life to facilitating spiritual opportunities for those seeking a greater understanding of their personal path. Her coordination of classes, workshops, and weekend events eventually led her to the founding of a non-profit interfaith community center devoted to those seeking their spirituality outside the mainstream traditions. Helping seekers find their way, she has served on various community-based non-profit boards. During her career, Maeven has also been active in the interfaith community on a local, state, and national level. She is currently a faculty member of the global spiritual community, Soul-Full.

Maeven's body of work has led her to appear in newspapers, magazine articles, television shows, documentaries, and books. She's passionate about all things community, as well as about gardening, foraging, and traveling with her soul mate.

Connect with Maeven:

Website: https://MagickalLife.com

Facebook: https://www.Facebook.com/MaevensMagickalLife/

Instagram: https://www.Instagram.com/MaevensMagickalLife/

Mystic Elements: https://mysticelements.com/collections/maeven-eller-five

Soul-Full: https://www.asoulfullworld.com

# CHAPTER 18

# THE SOUND OF SURRENDER

## THE ANCIENT ACT OF WAILING TO RELEASE PAIN, GRIEF, AND SUFFERING

Heather Southard

The room is dark except for the glowing candles on the altar table in the center of the circle. The leader of the ritual is wearing all black, walking around in a clockwise direction. She quietly leads us into a group "ohm" and then meditation. I'm sitting on my sleeping bag within the circle of other participants, each of us wrapped in our blankets or head scarves, focusing inward. I can feel anxiety in the room like a thick fog.

The wailing ritual taught me emotional turmoil is best healed by a radical, uninhibited, fierce feeling. Through wailing, these untethered, unruly, and messy emotions are released by cathartic tears without regret. Let me tell you how wailing helped me let go of decades of grief that were consuming me like a wild beast devouring its prize at the end of a hunt.

## MY STORY

As I settle into darkness, random thoughts run through my head. *I really should stop worrying. Relax and let the heart take over. Most people are mourning a recent loss. I don't know what I'm mourning. Why am I here at this moment?*

I trusted the individual leading the ritual and was willing to follow her lead.

"We're all going to start with some deep breathing and ohms. Make sure you're in a comfortable position. Take a deep breath in, and let's begin. Soft focus your eyes or close them. As you release your breath, use the sound ohm. Ohm. . . ohm. . ."

"Ohm. . .ohm. . ." At first, I was resisting, but slowly and eventually, I got swept up in the energy of the ohms. My head pulsated with the thrum of the ohms. As one ohm ended, another one began. "Ohm. . .Ohm. . ." I feel the ohms carry me deeper and deeper into my soul self.

The thrumming clears the fog, and I see myself standing at the rim of a great canyon. I take a step onto the path that leads down into it and find myself walking with ease, even though the path is rugged, with zig-zagging switchbacks. I'm floating along the path as I go deeper and deeper into the canyon.

*Wait, this place is familiar. I'm in the abyss.* The abyss is a place where I go in my deepest meditations. *How did I get here so quickly?*

"Let yourself settle into a place of deep relaxation and meditation, a place where you feel safe. This is a place and a time to let your emotions ebb and flow. You're safe to let it all go," she says. The calming words are pulling me deeper and more strongly than anything has ever pulled me in the past.

*I can't believe I've come here.* My abyss is a place of deep sorrow, but also comfort. In the past, I've come here many times—mostly to bury my deepest sadness. Where else but in a deep hole in the ground do you bury your worst emotions? This is where I've gone when I've hit rock bottom.

I step down off the last of the switchbacks as it empties onto the canyon floor. It's dusty and gravelly here. About ten feet in front of me is a cave composed of a flat boulder about ten feet across and two bigger rocks leaning against one another, each about 30 feet tall. This is where we played in my neighborhood, and why, as kids, we called it Big Rock. It's where we used to race to the top to prove ourselves. Inside the cave, which was more like an overhang, we used to find old bones of dead animals. In both meditation and real life, I'd go there when I was really sad and wanted to be alone.

But today I walk past Big Rock and the cave, going another 20 feet, where multiple paths begin and lead into shoots branching off the main canyon. There are numerous slot canyons, none of which I wish to visit tonight. I know where many of those go and they're not good memories.

If you could draw a map of all your memories so you'd know where they are to revisit later or to know where to avoid going again, wouldn't you? I have. Think of this as a canyon with many parallel slot canyons that all meander and join back to one another a few miles up the main canyon. There, at the end of all the paths, is a large dam holding the same water that formed these slots back when my soul was born.

Down one of the slots to the right, marked by a danger sign, is the imprisoned soul of one who harmed me in my youth. It's the soul of what some people call a demon. I trapped him in a cell so he could never cause harm again. In another slot is a black hole. It's where I've held on to the edge so as not to be sucked into the void. That's where I went when I'd hit rock bottom from suicidal depression.

There are also canyon slots filled with memorial stones representing loved ones who are now deceased. Each stone symbolizes unbearable grief. It's the canyon slot of buried sadness—grief deferred—another unquenched beast waiting for me around the next bend.

Yet other slots carry mixed emotional memories, such as happy past lives when I was a faery and lived in the realm of faeries and elves. It was sad when I had to leave that life. My faery family was in danger and they had to leave me in the human world where I'd be safer. That is my most recent past life which explains why I'm so connected to faery energy in this lifetime. Memories such as these are calling me, but I turn back toward Big Rock, choosing to stay in the main opening of the canyon this time.

*Listen to your emotions,* my inner voice of wisdom tells me. The dusty canyon floor stirs up these memories, making me choke. Raw emotions threaten to tear open my heart, aching from being broken too many times. In the canyon, the tears start to flow uninhibited, taking on a life of their own. Crying out, I can hear my heart beating, rushing in my ears. I can hear the rumbling of rushing water, and the ground begins to tremble.

*I know that sound. Oh shit! Here it comes.* Somewhere in the distance, my tears called forth the canyon waters, and the floodgate gave way. *There's nowhere to hide from what's about to happen. One cannot stop the voice of those old pains; those just unleashed like a wounded beast.*

Calling down from the rim of the canyon, returns the leader's voice, echoing the rolling thunder of the breaking dam. "Don't hold back your tears. Let them flow and wash it all away."

Back in the room, I'm called into awareness by the sounds of crying, wailing, moaning, and pounding on the floor. *Who's wailing and sobbing so loud? Oh, that's me.* My cries merge with theirs. As wailers, we are the sound of one heart breaking.

The waters from the dam come rushing down through multiple slot canyons and into the main canyon simultaneously. The waters in the abyss and the sounds in the room are one. Our wails ebb and flow as we ride the emotional waves together. As one person stops to breathe in a snotty breath, another one picks up the rhythm of wailing again. Like a giant wave, some of us are on the front end crashing down as others are cresting and riding the upsurge of emotions to its peak. We're in a never-ending wave pool. In a heartbeat, the waters sweep me off my feet. They deposit me on top of Big Rock, drenched in my tears and frayed straight to my core.

Once the wave subsided, I was able to catch my ragged breath. Exhausted and reeling with relief at the same time, I stood to look back through the canyon. To my surprise, I saw that only the canyon slots marked by danger signs were flooded out. And slowly the flood waters are receding like an outgoing tide. In their wake are some of the most beautiful, colorful flowers, growing at the entrance to the slots. The flood waters have quite literally left me with rainbows of color, and promises of new beginnings.

After about an hour, or what felt like an eternity in my abyss, the lights were slowly being turned on, and wailers began to stir, stretch, and awaken back to their current life. I'm back in the room on my sleeping bag. I'm thoroughly exhausted from the tsunami I just rode. At the same time, I feel a manic high from all the energy I just processed.

I dry off my tears, clean up my belongings, and join the others in the fellowship hall for snacks. There, we are encouraged to eat bread and chocolate and to rehydrate. Sometimes with the deep emotional work and energy flow this activates, one's mental body and physical body are disjointed from each other. Protein snacks help ground the energy, allowing one to reintegrate from the meditation psyche back into current reality. We're not allowed to leave until we assure the leader that we're back in our bodies, safe and sound.

For weeks after the ritual, I was aware of how I'd processed so many emotions without knowing to what occurrences they belonged. I've lost loved ones over the years, especially while in college, but I never fully processed those losses. I knew the catharsis of tears and being swallowed by the waves was transformative. I just couldn't name the grief. And let's acknowledge this—I didn't just release emotions; I was savagely devoured and spit back out. Grief is a relentless beast that pulls you everywhere, and it's messy, as there are no safe places to hide from it. Grief doesn't care about the process, only about the release.

Not until I was in my thirties did I truly understand how to grieve. In college, when I lost five people close to me, I didn't know what to do. I was stuck in a box with depression and only a constant class schedule to keep me afloat. I was in survival mode. During the wailing, I was able to release those losses—two family members, a family pet, and an online friend, who all died within six weeks of each other. That semester I was in a depressive fog. Even with being through therapy in college, I didn't know until the wailing how to fully process and release these deep and confusing emotions.

Flash forward eight years from my first wailing experience, and I had to go through grief all over again with the death of my mom. The wisdom I've gained from the wailing ceremonies helped me process this profound loss. I can now put a name to this transformation. Never underestimate the healing catharsis of tears and the heart-mending that takes place when we let go of the pain. It was through my introduction to the wailing that I truly came to understand the importance of grieving fiercely, without inhibitions and expectations.

The wailing helped me to better understand the beast called grief. It will still rear its ugly head, but I can now put a name to it and wrestle it till it surrenders. The wailing helped me process situations, disappointments, and grief in a way that was before unfathomable. Wailing can help you, too. Here are instructions for a personal wailing ritual, from which you too can find release.

# THE CEREMONY

## WAILING RITUAL

Sometimes in life, tears come easily, and sometimes they don't. This is one tool that may help you journey through the pain, named or unnamed, bringing up tears for catharsis and release. Remember that grief and the feeling of emotions are a way to know you're human. Grief is a superpower. The tears you experience help you move past pain instead of holding onto it to hurt yourself more.

### SET-UP:

When you prepare to do this ritual, let others around you know what you will be doing. For some, the wailing can be startling and loud. You wouldn't want people to check up on you part-way through and interrupt you, or worse, call the police. Set up space free from interruptions as much as you can. Do this ritual when you aren't on a schedule. Let it take whatever length of time feels necessary and complete, without feeling rushed. Wear loose clothing that allows for unencumbered movement and temperature comfort. Running this type of energy can cause both overheating and shivering. Be ready for both. You want to be in a room that is darkened from all light except for candlelight.

Assemble an altar with a black cloth full of candles and any items you wish to help represent your pain. This can include pictures, personal belongings, and artwork. In addition, place a few large rocks under your altar. These are for collecting all the negative emotions and energy you're about to release. Position plump pillows on the floor in your space, or have a comfortable chair ready. Other things to help bring about private space for a wailing are scarves and blankets to cover your head. These can help bring you deeper into yourself.

To set your sacred space, walk in a circle clockwise and use a broom to sweep out unwanted energy and bring in clean energy for protection. Call in guardians and elemental beings to help with energy movement. If this is not your tradition, pray from your own tradition. The purpose is to ask for those who bring you comfort to be there to keep you safe while you do this work.

When you feel your space is ready, get into a comfortable sitting or reclining position. Speak aloud your intentions for wailing and release. Understand that for this, there is no wrong way to wail. Feel free to cry out, yell, pound on the floor, roll into a ball, crawl around, pace, or rock back and forth. The only true advice for a wailing—don't hold back the tears intentionally, and don't judge them in the moment.

If you find it hard to cry, feel free to listen to sad music that has made you cry in the past. Otherwise, bring yourself into the wailing by sounding ohms, just like we did in the wailing I described above. Listen to others doing ohm chants if you wish.

Set your gaze to the candlelight on your altar. Use a soft focus to start your meditation. Clear your mind and let the sound and rhythm of the ohms carry you deep inside yourself. Take deep breaths in, and ohm on the out breaths. Let the ohms open your throat. Breathe into your heart and down into your belly, where we typically hold our pain in silence. Allow yourself to use sound to release pain—soft, loud, or fluctuating—do what feels best for your body at the moment.

Do not time yourself. When you feel complete in your release of emotions, bring yourself back to a comfortable position and controlled deep breathing. Take your time to come back to the present. As you come back into the room more mentally present, begin to stretch slowly, hug yourself, or tap yourself on both knees as you state your name aloud a few times. This helps bring you back into yourself fully.

Once you're ready to release the sacred space, thank all those who you called in to help you in the beginning and release them from their duty. To clear your space, walk counterclockwise with your broom or other tools useful for clearing. Turn on the lights and blow out the candles. For grounding and regaining energy, have bread, chocolates, cheeses, nuts, or other light protein snacks. Rehydrate with plenty of water or other non-caffeinated beverage.

Do not rush back into daily activities. Take it easy for the rest of the day. Journal or do artwork about your experience to help finish processing what emotions arose. If necessary, find someone to talk to about your experience. Know that you have released all that is not for your higher good. Within 24 hours, bury the rocks that were under your altar. Let the earth neutralize this energy you've released.

The final step after a wailing ritual is to congratulate yourself. You've faced fears and emotions that take courage. Remember that you're human and it's a messy thing to be sometimes. Never let the beast of grief, pain, and suffering wrestle you into submission. Let this wailing help loosen the pain, releasing you from the beast and bringing you a rainbow from the tears.

I hope you find how freeing a wailing can be.

**Heather Southard,** in her childhood, always dreamed of helping people and saving animals and the planet, probably by being a vet, a superhero, a writer, or all of the above. She loved reading, volunteering, raising money for charity with her youth group, and decorating with peace signs. It is no wonder she now loves all those things while working in the non-profit sector helping differently-abled people. She also finds fulfillment as an active member of two religious houses of worship, working her superhero skills teaching the youth, and doing multiple social justice activities. Heather lives with her husband, teenage son, and a feisty feline in Colorado Springs, Colorado. In her free time, when she is not out helping save the world, she loves reading, cross-stitching, quilting, hiking, and writing rituals, meditations, poems, and short stories. If you have questions about the Wailing Ritual or would like her to write personalized rituals for you, please email her at hssouthard@outlook.com.

# CHAPTER 19

# THE JOURNEY WITHIN

## AWAKENING YOUR OWN SPIRITUAL DIVINITY

Misty Dawn Shakti Sharma, RN

*"Almighty and Eternal Fount of Wisdom...*
*Grant us knowledge, understanding, and wisdom to speak here*
*words of Truth, Love, and Hope... May those who are now in*
*darkness and obscurity, be brought into the radiant sunshine and*
*the joyous glory of the unfoldment of true spiritual goodness."*

~ Ding Le Mei

## MY STORY

I was flying. Well, that's what it felt like. I wasn't in my body; I was pure energy moving. I saw grass and the sky as I flew. Flying is the only word I can think of, though it felt much slower. I felt like I was existence in slow motion, and I was seeing how life began. Not only how it began, but also what it felt like to be pure life. I was the wind. And then I was the spider spinning a web. All at once I came back into awareness and felt myself sitting on the warm, plush carpet. I was in Joshua Tree, California, at the Institute of Mentalphysics. My teacher had just led us through the Eight Key Breaths of Ding Le Mei. The little building we were in was named the Lotus Meditation Building, and it became my sanctuary, my church.

I slowly opened my eyes, *I don't want to come back,* I thought. It felt so good to be free from my body, my attachments, and pure energy form. I recognized that the meditation I just experienced showed me, visually and through the movement of energy, that there is a Divinity in everything— the wind, the spider, and her web. I felt I was now seeing the world through awakened eyes.

## OUT OF DESTRUCTION COMES REBIRTH

Finally, it's over. My divorce was finalized. I felt free. I felt like I was breathing again. I didn't realize how much my energy was being sucked from me. I felt alive in a new way that is hard to describe. Not only had this toxic relationship been laid to rest, but I also graduated from nursing school. After six years, I could finally breathe. I looked around the tiny trailer I was living in with my children, grateful for its protection, but wanting to manifest a home with more windows and brightness. I remember when it struck me, and I realized my life was a direct manifestation of my thoughts and the main vibrations I carried. At the time, it was a painful realization, not because there wasn't any good, but because there was so much not serving me. I decided at that moment that I'd do my best to create a life that was a reflection of my soul and spirit, not just to survive but to thrive. *I'll begin again, right now;* I silently prayed.

The house I manifested has three bedrooms and an extra room *to do Yoga,* I thought. It is bright and cheery, with yellow-painted walls, and many windows that let in the light.

I fell to my knees in gratitude and bowed my head, as a river of tears fell. The kind of tears that feel so good when they come. It took so much work and sacrifice to get to this moment. I thought back to the young 17-year-old me who found herself carrying life. I remember a moment when I was watching an educational program about pregnancy, and I was crying. My son kicked at that precise moment as if saying, "I'm here Mom, don't cry. You are not alone." As I stretched out on my yoga mat in the bright yellow room in my new house, I entered into the Cobra pose and felt the most delicious vibrations throughout my body. "Ahh," I moaned with the pleasure and intensity of it all, stretching and feeling my spirit within my beautiful body like never before. I made friends with my body in a new and sacred way.

If I reflect, I've always been a deep thinker—a spiritual person. I had a longing to understand, and a yearning for the mysteries to be revealed. I don't know that I've had full consciousness of this. The transition from a teenager to an adult occurred quickly for me. And so I began a journey to make something of myself, to survive, but also ultimately to thrive. The need to survive and keep going can be compared to contractions as one labors. There is a moment in labor where you're deep within yourself; it's you and the rawness of life. As my spirit awakened, I felt like I had arrived, birthing a new consciousness. I was the fruit ripening for the spiritual experiences that would touch me to my core and shape the rest of my life.

## AFTER SURVIVAL MODE COMES REST

There was a point after so much struggle where, for the first time after becoming a young mother, I had enough—enough finances and enough time to begin to look at filling my own spiritual cup. My two sons were in elementary school, and I utilized that time to explore. I was looking outside of myself for healing. I was always an open person who enjoyed different cultures, and this would be helpful to me as I journeyed deeper than I thought possible. Staying open is not just a suggestion but can be a way of life. I believe my education as a nurse helped ripen me for further expansion with spirit because it taught me to be open-minded.

## IT STARTED SIMPLE AND SMALL

When we think of awakening, or rites and rituals, sometimes we think it needs to be this large moment, a comet of awareness. But if I trace it back, I see it's a small moment where I took myself out to explore. It felt like I was going outward but really what I did was go inward. I was opening after so long. I learned recently that my favorite tree, the Mimosa tree, has leaves that close in response to being touched, due to sensitivity. I've felt this way too. But now I was opening to the touch of the Divine.

On an ordinary Tuesday, I went to a café in Joshua Tree, with my new book. *This is the peace I'm missing,* I thought as I drank my green juice. *This feels so good.* I learned to take care of myself and recognize I'm a soul. It sounds simple and small, but for someone who went through many years of adversity, struggle, and survival, it was huge!

I still remember this day; seven years later, I can still climb into the memory. There was a flow I experienced. Some might call this Divine orchestration or Divine flow—synchronicity, manifestation. I didn't know any of these terms then; I only knew it felt so good!

On this day, I flowed. I went to different places around my community and allowed myself to show up as my authentic, sensitive, wandering soul. I wandered without an agenda. I was open to the good, and the possible. On this most auspicious day, I found out about a class at the Institute of Mentalphysics in Joshua Tree. I had driven by the institute my whole life and always been intrigued, but never had I inquired. For some reason, I now recognize as fate. It felt like the right time. And now I found a class, The Eight Key Breaths of Ding Le Mei, Tuesday evenings, from 6:30 p.m. to 8 p.m. I wrote it down in my small notebook. I went to that class for the first time expecting nothing, not knowing my life would change. I was catapulted into the biggest spiritual awakening of my life. I journeyed through Kundalini awakening and self-discovery. I became a more complete version of my highest self.

## THE SACREDNESS OF BREATH
## AT THE LOTUS MEDITATION BUILDING

I came to the Institute of Mentalphysics, a massive property located in Joshua Tree, California, in the Southern California Mojave Desert. I lived only a short distance away, in Twentynine Palms. You can make out parts of the property from the road, trees peeking out, like parts of a mystery exposed. I felt scared and awkward, jumpy, and anxious. *I'm scared I will get lost and won't know my way,* I thought. I'd felt like this a lot lately.

I went to the main office and received directions to the Lotus Meditation Building. In the main courtyard, there was a golden statue of Buddha. He seemed so light, so free, smiling with the answers to secrets. There was a bell above his head; *I wonder what it would be like to ring that bell loudly for all to hear!* But instead, I made my way to a small courtyard with water. I was still nervous, waiting for the teacher to come. There were a few people in the courtyard with me. The teacher arrived and I introduced myself, "Hi, I'm Misty," I said, "I'm here for the class." My teacher looked at me with eyes that seemed to pierce through all my defenses, and peer directly into my soul. My teacher was my first encounter with a spiritual man, who knew himself and seemed to have complete sovereignty of his being. And though we had just met, our souls knew this was not the first time.

We entered the Lotus Meditation Building, a small building with lush purple velvet carpets and three triangles forming windows. I chose to sit directly on the floor, not knowing then how much I needed grounding. My teacher walked us through the Eight Key Breaths of Ding Le Mei. This was the first time in my life I was consciously aware of my sacred breath. I never focused on my breath. My teacher's voice was calming, grounding, and strong—exactly the energy I needed to be around. It gave me the support and courage to keep breathing. I was 25 years old. This was the first time, besides a yoga class I took in college, where I meditated, stopped, and sat with myself with no agenda or to-do list.

Going from small wimpy breaths to inhaling deep gulps of air is a high. It can make you feel all-powerful, and it can also drop you to your knees, making you feel faint. Most of us do not breathe deeply, but rather live on shallow breaths. My teacher said, "I want you to recognize there is an innate spirit inside you, an intelligent life force that keeps you breathing. This breath is sacred." As a nurse, I understood how the respiratory system works, and how complex the human body is. But I found myself thinking: *Wow! It's my spirit that keeps me breathing.*

After class, I stayed and talked with my teacher. He discussed Astrology. I remember listening to him intently, my whole being recognizing this moment before my mind or consciousness ever would. I remember time fading, and the structures of objects around me fading too. I experienced an alchemical moment where Spirit is raw and pure. It was a destiny-filled moment. I arrived at this moment. And even though a short while ago I was afraid, I no longer was.

To say that class changed my life is no understatement. To say it saved my life is a fact. To say it helped awaken my soul is the truth.

Sometimes rites and rituals look big—a fire ceremony, being baptized in water. But for me, it happened in the slow and steady breath, in the slowing down, in the ritual of coming to the Institute of Mentalphysics every Tuesday for a year to breathe. By learning to breathe I experienced so much energy and learned about Prana, our essential life force. As the breath began to balance my body, mind, and soul I was led to other gifts. By remaining open to the journey, I experienced many miracles. This was not a scientific awakening; as a nurse, I knew what good oxygenation does for a body. But I awakened to the part of me the world suppressed, and that I also pushed down and away. I awakened to my soul.

Things began to flow through me through intuition and meditation. For example, I was raised Christian and never heard about the Hindu god Shiva or Goddess Shakti. Through these breaths, I learned that Lord Shiva represents the Divine Masculine, the consciousness. Shakti represents the Divine Feminine and raw energy. Energy without consciousness spins idly. And consciousness without energy to experience sits idly. It's the balance of both masculine and feminine energy carried in us that helps us live a more balanced life.

Once I experienced this divine flow of intuitive information, it became easier to allow myself to be open to the Divine and explore information that came through to my soul. You may call this channeling or prayer. Many names work. As I allowed myself to flow with the Divine, I recognized I was diving deep into the mysteries of the Universe. The mysteries that used to scare me now intrigued me. I'm still flowing with this ritual of intuitive downloading and tapping into the Divine. My mindset switched from, *the Universe is a scary, fearful place,* to my mantra, *the Universe surprises me with its mysteries.* Rites and rituals may not always be something big, but rather something small that is begging to be explored and borne witness to.

How often does a soft moment come as a reminder that worlds are birthed from breath? Do not underestimate the power of beginning, exploring, or of taking that first step and trying something new.

As I became more awakened, I became deeply aware of the moon's presence in my life. It was as if I was seeing her for the first time, though I knew I was seeing her through newly awakened eyes and consciousness.

One of the things I learned about was working with the moon for manifestation and healing. I learned that you could release by the full moon and manifest by planting seeds on the new moon. One of the ways you can do this is by writing.

As a young girl, I loved Shakespeare and used to write songs and poems. At some point in my life, I stopped. During this awakening, I started writing again—a thought, sentence, or page to express what I was experiencing. I began to write again by the moon. The ritual of following the full moon and new moon became a comfort for me. I wrote in a certain style. When releasing by the full moon, I started by writing the words, "I release what no longer serves me in the highest good for myself." During this time, I reflected on whatever I felt was no longer serving my highest good. This could be an attachment, thought, or experience. It is powerful to name it.

Writing it down on paper made it more concrete. After writing it, you can rip it into pieces or burn it—whatever works for you.

By the new moon, I had a chance to create and manifest. I had nothing to lose by trying this, and so I wrote as if the thing I was asking for, was already occurring. I manifested many things, big and small, this way. And it changed my way of thinking. I went to a local art show and saw a vase with Shiva doing the Tandava—The dance of Destruction and Creation. In a sense, my awakening was the unraveling, or destruction, if you will, of what no longer served me. My awakening was also the rebirth of my soul. This Shiva jar became my manifestation jar before I knew what a manifestation jar was. I began to hold my new moon manifestations within my Shiva jar.

# THE CEREMONY

## CREATE YOUR OWN MANIFESTATION JAR

Look for an object that means something to you and that you can store your notes in. It should be something that is of your own energy, and something that inspires you and brings you peace and joy.

Look up the date of the next full moon. Reflect on what you want to release. Think about what is no longer serving you. What would it be like to release the heaviness of what you're carrying? Write it down. Once written, rip it, shred it, or burn it, but do let it go, let it flow, and allow it to heal. Take a breath, and exhale, releasing what no longer serves you.

At the new moon, write down the seeds you want to plant. What do you want to nourish in your life? What do you want to come to fruition? Keep this in your manifestation jar. Take a new breath and believe.

Now that you have completed the ritual, the rite is faith, and being the vibrational match to what you want to plant. Do you believe in what you're doing? Are you connected to it? Can you hold space and faith for it to grow? Anyone who has ever grown something from a seed to a plant knows it's something sacred. Allowing yourself the time and space to grow will allow you to nourish that sacredness, all while you remember the sacredness of your breath and of your soul.

As you start to experience your manifestations, do, from time to time, take out your notes from your manifestation jar to read. Become aware of your journey, and foster gratitude for the Divine that helps nourish your manifestations. Gratitude is the key to manifesting. Do sit with yourself and breathe, feeling your divine soul resting in your being.

**Misty Dawn Shakti Sharma** is a registered nurse, writer, poetess, mystic, motivational speaker, spiritual consultant, and mentor in spiritual thought practice. Her poetry and writing are a way to introduce spiritual thought practice as holistic support to those searching for more meaning in their lives. She has experience working in population health, community health, mental health, pain management, trans-disciplinary care, geriatrics, and holistic nursing. Misty currently serves as an elected official on the Morongo Basin Healthcare District Board of Directors. She believes that healthcare is a human right as she serves to advocate for others. Misty is the author of the book, *Memoirs of My Divination,* meaning the memories of her journey to find God. Her book is a poetry collection that tells her own journey of soul awakening and inspires others through spiritual thought practice. Misty is the host of the podcast, *Kavi Heart,* which takes a poetic perspective of journeying through life's mysteries. She would love to connect with you.

Connect with Misty:

Linktree: https://linktr.ee/MistyDawnShaktiShama

Facebook: https://www.facebook.com/mistydawnshaktisharma

Instagram: Misty Dawn Shakti Sharma (@mistydawnshaktisharma) • Instagram photos and videos

Website: Desert Risings by Misty Dawn Shakti Sharma

LinkedIn: Misty (Evans) Sharma | LinkedIn

Resource: Institute of Mentalphysics – Joshua Tree Retreat Center (jtrcc.org)

# CHAPTER 20

# I MARRIED MYSELF

## A CEREMONY OF SELF-LOVE, COMMITMENT, AND INTEGRATION

Tina Green

## MY STORY

It's a chilly spring night in Teotihuacan, Mexico. I'm sitting in the dimly-lit, still-vibrant dining room at the Dreaming House, an enclosed family compound created to host groups on transformational journeys steeped in Toltec wisdom. I'm in the middle of a week-long shamanic retreat, and everyone else in the group has retired to their rooms.

I sit alone, sipping a mug of hot mint tea, contemplating the changes in my life over recent months, and what I've truly overcome.

*I used to let so many people's opinions and judgments take root in me.*

*I judged and rejected myself constantly.*

*I was so overwhelmed, resentful, and lonely.*

There was so much about myself and my young life that I denied and minimized. There was abandonment, neglect, sexual abuse, disrespect, and the deeply-seated agreements that came along with them so I could cope as a child.

I created the story that my childhood was beautiful. Yes, there were many terrific moments, and my family loved me and did their best. This isn't about blame; it's about being truthful and getting back those parts of my soul that went away. It's about healing.

When I was ready to expose the roots of my low self-esteem and body shame, I discovered that I wasn't telling the truth about my childhood. I became a master of denial and minimization. This story worked brilliantly to help me cope and move forward as a child, but now it was just holding me back and keeping me in pain.

As a child, I took in all the information from my environment, and I agreed to it. I didn't have a choice; it's what I was taught. I created a set of unconscious agreements that would be the foundation of my operating system. This is how I successfully got my needs met as a child. These agreements worked well at the time, but as an adult, many of them no longer serve me.

Healing began by acknowledging that my family provided almost no emotional support or intimacy. Therefore, when things happened, like sexual abuse by a family member when my parents were not home, I created agreements around how men respect me and my body.

When my dad moved out without telling me when I was 15, and moved in with his mistress and her daughter, I made more agreements about how men respect my mom and me, how I don't matter, and how I need to behave to get the love and approval of my father.

When my sibling punched me and put me down all the time, I created more agreements about how I'm not enough, I don't matter, men don't respect me, and men are better than me.

When I was 12, and my girlfriend's younger brother peeped at me while I was changing, and exclaimed to all my friends, "Wow, she is fat!" my body shame became stronger, and I created the agreements that boys aren't attracted to me and don't respect me.

When I was 17, and my boyfriend shared intimate details about me with his friends, and I became a joke to them, and one of them said to me, "You're a waste of a life," it further solidified my body shame and my agreements that men don't respect me. I'm not enough, and I don't matter.

When I was told as a toddler, "Don't ever touch your crotch; it's dirty!" I created agreements of shame around my body.

Most of all, when all of the teenage social dynamics happened, I had no one to talk to. I dealt with situations poorly because I wasn't shown or taught how to be in healthy relationships, take care of my body, and how to talk about hard things.

Once I could acknowledge these agreements, feel the anger and sadness, release them from my body, and make new agreements, I could truly love myself. It has been quite a healing journey that has included counseling, Toltec Sacred Journey Breathwork, ceremony, initiation, writing, and group sharing. I both welcomed and resisted the healing. I set powerful intentions, told the truth, screamed, sobbed, breathed, and felt the pain I stuffed down in my body.

All this was necessary for me to heal and feel the freedom I feel now.

*Those old agreements are no longer ruling my life!*

*I'm so grateful that I now love and accept myself.*

*That was the answer all along!*

Now, I'm ready to take the next step in my healing. Earlier today, when we returned from a day of powerful teaching and initiations at the Pyramids of Teotihuacan, our teachers gave us an assignment, "Tomorrow, we will invite you to participate in a sacred marriage ceremony. You will be marrying and making a lifelong commitment to yourself."

I was immediately excited! We all looked at each other and smiled.

He continued, "You will need to spend some time tonight writing your vows."

*This is perfect! I've already released so much pain and barriers, and I now truly love myself, and because of that, I finally feel whole. I'm so ready for this! I want to carry this love with me for the rest of my life.*

*Feeling whole.*

*That feels so good. My soul is home.*

Since I was a young girl, I thought feeling whole and happy came from marrying a man and having children. This is how I was trained. Now I understand that nothing outside of myself can make me feel whole. It has to come from within.

*Okay, I need to focus on writing my vows now.*

Still sitting in the dimly lit dining room with festive papel picados (ceremonial flags) hanging from the ceiling, I'm trying to create my vows, and my mind is blank.

*I can't believe I can't come up with anything! Come on, Tina! I thought this would be easy!*

*Okay, I guess I will have to Google it to get me started. Let's start with "marriage to myself."*

I quickly peruse through the results.

*Hmm. None of these captures how I truly want to make this commitment. These vows are all so general and based on tradition. I want to break tradition and get specific to my healing journey.*

*Maybe I'll just start writing in my journal about what this means to me.*

As I'm writing, it strikes me to make an inventory of my healed wounds or agreements (abandonment, neglect, sexual abuse, body shame, I'm not enough, I don't matter, relationship with men) and my sacred longings (self-love, spirituality, love, respect, no fear).

*Okay, this is a start. Now let's see if I can come up with something!*

I start writing, crossing out, rewriting, and rewriting again until I finally feel that my vows are complete.

*I am exhausted. That was a big day. It's time to give it a rest and go to bed.*

After an unusually deep and restorative sleep, I awake, stretch, and rise.

*Oh right! It's my wedding day! Yay!*

I grab my journal and start reading my vows again.

*Hmm…this still doesn't feel right to me. It's missing something. It doesn't go deep enough.*

I read them out loud multiple times, and then it hit me.

*Of course! It's missing spirituality. My new-found spirituality is so vital to the new me.*

While I stepped away from my Catholic religion years ago because of the oppressive view of women, I've always craved spirituality, and I now have it. I now connect deeply with the divine mother as my higher power. She has visited me on multiple occasions to assure me that she loves me unconditionally and is always with me. I pray to her, and she guides my soul. Now, I feel the nurturing mother's love, and I never feel alone.

I write spirituality into my vows, and now, they're complete.

As I get dressed for the day, I feel the fluttering of excited butterflies in my chest and a glow of love emanating from me.

*This ceremony is my most significant commitment—after all the healing and transformation I've experienced, this is an affirmation of unconditional love from within and an eternal commitment to my soul. These are my new roots.*

When it was time for my sacred marriage ceremony, I approached the space we lovingly call "The Womb." It's a teaching salon where we meet as a group to learn, share, cry, laugh, scream, breathe, and hug. On one end of the room is a mural painting of the Virgen de Guadalupe, and throughout the space is sacred artwork, hand-carved stone sculptures, drums, mirrors, and comfortable couches. I have had so many holy experiences in this space. This is where I found spirituality, gave my shame back to my ancestors, learned how to tell my truth, and learned how to love myself. Now, this is where I will make my sacred commitment to myself!

*This is going to be a powerful experience!*

My intent was already working.

One of my teachers smudged me with the smoke from the burning copal, a resin from the tree of life. This is an ancient practice used to cleanse the energy and invite in positive energy.

I take a deep breath.

*Divine mother, ancestors, eagle, and red birds, please join me and be my sacred witness.*

With reverence, I slowly open the door and step into the womb. It takes my breath away.

A path of rose petals leads me to a beautiful altar with the centerpiece being a mirror. The altar sits in front of the mural of the Virgen de Guadalupe that I have connected with so deeply.

I sit on a pillow and gaze at myself in the mirror.

Flowers surround me. In front of me are red roses, and on either side, the room is filled with colorful, fragrant flowers, and among the flowers are candles and angels.

Soft ethereal music is playing, and my nose fills up with the nectar of the flowers combined with the burning, energy-clearing copal.

"I love you."

My face and eyes change and soften.

I smile.

*I am so beautiful.*

I feel a calm come over me.

With my teachers, higher power, ancestors, guides, and fellow journeyers as my sacred witnesses, I continue to gaze into the mirror, take a deep breath, and declare my vows:

"I will love myself as if I were my own child.

I will consider my body sacred and nourish it with love, movement, and good food.

I will surround myself with people who love, value, and respect me.

I will give myself love, comfort, and grace.

When hard things happen, I will ask for help.

I will not let fear or voices from the past stand in the way of becoming the person I was meant to be.

I will continue to look to my soul, the divine mother, and the great mystery to guide me in painting the grand masterpiece that is my life."

I smile, take a deep breath, gaze into my eyes and say softly, "I love you, Tina."

With a big smile and a glow in my heart, I stand up and turn around to face my witnesses. They cheered, showered me with rose petals, and hugged me.

I giggle with delight.

I feel a sense of inner peace and joy.

*I finally feel guided from within by my soul instead of my ego or any outside expectations.*

As I witness the others in their ceremony, I have tears streaming down my cheeks. Everyone's vows are beautiful and tailored to their unique life journey.

For days, I floated around with a euphoric feeling in my chest. I can only describe it as universal love. My capacity for love has transformed and grown significantly.

This ceremony continues to be a potent moment in my life that I go back to often. I have my vows hanging in my home office. I revisit them when I'm having a tough day; it feels very grounding to read them, drop into my heart, and feel that deep commitment to my soul.

I believe that every human would benefit from participating in this ceremony. I imagine how it might change our world if every young person were to commit to themselves in this way before moving into their adult life. The practice of loving oneself first before committing to another is so powerful—and having the knowing that you cannot find wholeness from anything outside of yourself could change so much in our human dynamics. In my case, it took over 50 years for me to get to this point of self-love. This ceremony and my vows have been an important step in that journey to keep me in that love and remind me of my commitment to myself above all else.

# THE CEREMONY

You can create a Sacred Marriage Ceremony for yourself. As with any ceremony, it takes intention, thought, and planning. You'll need a journal or a notebook and a pen.

The most important thing to remember is to create the ceremony you want. Not the one that'll impress others. Check in about every decision, and ask: *Is this what I want, or is this what I think someone else expects?*

Your ceremony can range from very simple to elaborate. If you want a simple ceremony, there are four essential items: a mirror, an altar, vows, and at least one witness.

What would make this ceremony beautiful, meaningful, and powerful? That's for you to determine. Here are some suggested questions and possibilities you can ask yourself. If a question doesn't resonate with you, then skip it, and move on to the next possibility:

1. Where do you want to hold the ceremony?
2. What is your vision for the altar?
3. Do you want flowers? If so, what are your favorite flowers?
4. Do you have candles, or would you like to purchase special ones?
5. What sacred items do you want to include on the altar?
6. What do you want to wear?
7. Will there be a ring or another piece of jewelry that will symbolize your marriage?
8. Do you want to sit, kneel or stand? Is there a particular chair or pillow?
9. Do you want music playing? If so, what music?
10. Who will be your witness or witnesses?

Vows:

1. Start with a list of your most important values.
2. Add what you most want for yourself. What are your sacred longings?
3. Add a list of wounds or traumas you're tending to or have healed.
4. Use this list to inform your creation of your vows.
5. Write your vows, and revisit them several times over a day or two. Have a copy with you for the ceremony. No need to memorize them.

Now you can put together your final plan. I recommend giving yourself space after the ceremony to celebrate by doing something you love with people you love or just being.

Remember, this is for you, so there is no wrong way to do it. Give yourself exactly what you want without compromise.

For inspiration, if you want to see photos and vows from my sacred marriage, go to www.exposingtheroots.com/sacredmarriage.

I hope you have a beautiful ceremony that empowers you to live the life of your dreams, and I hope your vows can ground you in your commitment for the rest of your life.

**Tina Green** is the "Self-Love Queen," and she is the Founder, Owner, and Transformational Coach at Exposing The Roots.

Through her coaching, Toltec Sacred Journey Breathwork, rituals, women's circles, and retreats, Tina partners with women to increase their self-love. She is especially passionate about women loving their bodies!

Tina believes that when a woman learns to love herself, everything changes and anything is possible.

Tina is an ordained Minister of the Healing Arts, Toltec Sacred Journey Breathwork Facilitator, #1 Best-Selling Author, trained Life Coach, and Chef. She brings her vital mother energy and lived experience to everyone she serves. She also has 20 years of experience as an executive in non-profit and financial services.

Tina lives with her husband and two teenage daughters in Northern California. She is a personal transformation enthusiast, life-long student, foodie, outdoor adventurer, music and theatre lover, and traveler.

Connect with Tina:

Website: https://www.ExposingTheRoots.com

Facebook: https://www.facebook.com/ExposingTheRoots

Instagram: https://www.Instagram.com/ExposingTheRoots

Email: Tina@ExposingTheRoots.com

Phone: 707-872-7706

# CHAPTER 21

# CONVERSATIONS WITH DEATH

## BEFRIENDING THE GRIM REAPER THROUGH DAILY PRACTICES

Rev. Mark J. Platten, MBA

## MY STORY

It's the summer of 2000, and the solstice is just around the corner, beckoning me with its searing heat and extended days. I heed the call and gently unfold the aging Colorado map with its faded names and torn edges, laying it across the kitchen table like an oracle.

"Great Spirit, guide me to the sacred location where I should take my next quest," I speak in reverent tones looking upward so I can receive.

I close my eyes, center myself, and place my hand approximately an inch from the surface of the map, moving slowly across its contents, searching for the *pull*, the visceral, magnetic-like draw that lets me know I have found the place. After several minutes, my index finger grazes the surface. I open my eyes and see I'm being guided to the Lake San Isabel area for this inner quest, my blend of the Native American vision quest, Buddhism, shamanic work, and various Earth-based traditions.

I've been going on seasonal quests for the past four years and am always amazed at the different messages they offer. I've learned to set aside expectations and just be in the moment, paying attention to the insights and guidance from Spirit. These come in many forms including animals, dreams, meditations, shamanic journeys, and sacred fire work.

I'll fast the entire time, which allows me to connect with Spirit more deeply. Food can be a strong physical and emotional distraction. It's as important to empty the physical vessel as it is for the mental, emotional, and spiritual bodies, to receive the messages with clarity and clear interpretation.

I head south, leaving Colorado Springs behind, and notice two ravens sitting on adjacent fence posts, looking at me. Raven is one of my primary totem animals, so I take this as a good omen that I'm in alignment with the quest.

I approach the area where my finger alighted on the map and open my heart for guidance. I see it. A sign that says, "Second Mesa Trail." I've been working with Native American teachers, so it's a clear sign. Further down the Forest Service Road, I see the sign again, only this time it says, "Second *Mace* Trail!" I laugh at this heyoka (sacred clown or trickster energy from the Sioux tradition) trick, but trust Spirit is guiding me.

I park, lock the doors, and use the key to open the trunk. It squeaks in defiance as I place my right arm through the strap of the 55-pound pack and, in one fluid motion, sling it onto my back, then adjust the weight between my shoulders and hips.

The first mile is steep, which adds to the physical stress of starting at 9,000 feet. The granite regolith crunches with each step I take and soon becomes a meditative encounter as sweat pours down my face. *I should have left earlier. I'm hot and uncomfortable and don't want to run out of daylight like in the winter quest where I almost died.*

I feel the land and sense the nature spirits, paying attention to their guidance. A couple of places have promise, but I keep getting the message to continue. Around four miles in, I spot a plateau with a rock outcropping. I drop my pack in case it's not the right place. Once the pack is released, I feel like I'm floating as I scramble up the hill. The site is perfect: trees for shade, a large opening for a fire circle, and the rock outcrop for meditating.

"Spirits of the land, may I set up sacred space and connect with you over the next four days?" I ask reverently. I wait for a few seconds and then my body is pulled forward strongly, in a deep bow. This is the somatic response I'm waiting for, something that Spirit has used to communicate with me for the past eight years.

I retrieve the pack and lug it up the final incline. I open a side zipper, pull out some organic tobacco, and make an offering to the spirits of the land. Next, I set up an altar for the spirits and the nature spirits of the site. I establish the energetic boundaries of the container, call in the elementals and directions, and offer gratitude.

An hour before sunset, I feel the call to create the sacred fire circle. I take deep breaths through my nose, release through my mouth, soften my eyes, open to receive, and sing to the elements as I conduct this task.

"O sacred stone of the earth element, let yourself be known to me that you may anchor the earth energy and ground our fire circle," I sing while searching for the stone. I continue the chant until I feel drawn to a particular stone.

"Will you be part of the sacred circle and hold the energy of earth?" I ask, waiting for its response.

*Yes, I would be honored to anchor the north and be part of the sacred fire circle. Thank you for asking.*

I do the same with each cardinal direction until reaching east—the water element. For some reason, I couldn't find the stone. Then, I hear it. A faint whisper to the east. I focus my attention and recognize the soft *woosh* of water from a mountain stream. The appropriate stone makes itself known and I complete the cardinal directions and then fill the gaps with other stones that want to be part of the circle.

"Standing Ones, guide me to the branches and kindling that want to be transmuted by the fire and become part of the ceremony," I speak to the trees. I collect their offerings, then wait.

I feel the energy shift and know it's time to light the fire. Just as with gathering the stones, I always sing the fire awake. Only tonight, something is different. I lean over the kindling to start my fire song, and instead of beginning the song, I receive a message. *Tonight, we want you to have a dark fire and receive the gifts it has to offer.*

"What is a dark fire, and why do I need to do one tonight?" I ask inquisitively.

*You will sing the fire awake as you always do, but you will light it with your intention and not the physical flame. This will allow you to access truths only the Darkness can offer.*

I spent a lot of time creating the circle and gathering kindling and firewood, and I was looking forward to the sacred flames of transmutation to help me answer some of the questions weighing on my heart. I'm frustrated by the request, but trust the message and do as instructed, singing the fire awake without lighting it. I feel it light as a wave of energy flows from the ethereal fire in a subtle, mysterious way, as though it holds secrets.

I grab my Buffalo frame drum and wake it up as I offer the sacred tobacco, circling three times in a clockwise manner above its face.

"Awaken brother drum and guide me with your rhythm and song around this sacred fire," I speak while my right hand completes three clockwise circles on the face of the drum, swirling the tobacco. I raise it to my heart and connect as I'm permitted to drum while I chant and dance around the fire.

The outside observer wouldn't make out many words, just sounds arising from within me as I surrender and become the vessel, the instrument played by the fire and Spirit. I circumambulate the fire, enter a trance state, and notice plant, animal, and nature spirit energies. Some are familiar and join in, while others stand at the perimeter and observe. Most often I sense a shape and its energy form, but occasionally I'm shown more and can physically see them, although in a translucent state.

*What is the purpose of the dark fire? Did I just make this up? No, I heard the message, but this is strange, even for me.*

I continue circling and chanting until I come to an abrupt stop. There are no more words, chants, or sounds coursing through me. I am the open and empty vessel, ready to receive. I'm disoriented from the trancelike state and need to ground my energy.

*We invite you to lie upon the earth and let her cradle and comfort you as you surrender control and allow the visions to arise.*

I do as instructed, choosing a spot close to the fire circle. I lie face up, close my eyes, and open to the unknown. I soften and relax, embracing the cool, slightly damp earth, as I enter a deep, meditative state and am aware of sitting in complete darkness, waiting. After a few minutes, something arises. Another shade of black against the night, subtly different, but there.

I'm transfixed as it moves toward me, tracking its movement because if it stopped, it would disappear into the surrounding darkness. *What is it? Why doesn't it show itself?*

The anticipation and uncertainty feel like an eternity. The closer it gets, the more it materializes and becomes a discernable, humanoid form. It's wearing a dark cloak and appears to be well over seven feet tall. The energy is masculine, and although I cannot see his face, the eyes have a piercing quality to them that demands respect and exudes power. I rise as he approaches.

"Who are you?" I ask when he's within a few yards of me. Part of me is observing the power which radiates from him, while another part is curious why I'm not the least bit afraid.

"You would call me Death, although I'm much more than your limited understanding," he responds in a deep but comforting tone.

"Why are you here tonight? Hopefully, it's not my time to go."

"You know I'm not here to escort you. Stand in your power. You are ready to learn important knowledge about me because you will someday write about the process humans call death, and I need you to understand who I am," he exclaimed with a bit of frustration at my pettiness.

The longer we talk, the more comfortable I feel, as though he were an old friend. In some regard, I guess he is.

"I would like for you to come with me and meet someone I'm guiding to the other side," he said more as a command than a choice.

I followed his skyward look and saw a large, winged creature coming toward us.

*A black pegasus? How cliché!*

I don't recall Death mounting the pegasus; he just appears on its bare back, reaches down, grabs my hand, and pulls me up behind him. I'm surprised. His hand is strong, solid, and warm. Not what I expected. We take off in the pitch-black night, and even though it seems like we're going extremely fast, I don't notice a breeze or feel any movement except for the pegasus' muscles rippling with each wingbeat.

After what seems like only a few minutes, we descend toward a young girl—no more than seven—with long, blond hair, who is standing alone in a field. She looks a bit disheveled, as though she just woke up, and glances in our direction without much expression. That changes as we come closer, her placid demeanor transitioning to one of fear and apprehension.

My heart sinks and courage pulses through my body, needing to protect her. She must have noticed Death coming to take her from the land of the living. I prepare to get between him and the girl as soon as we land so I can plead for her life and fight him if necessary. As the pegasus lands, she turns to Death and smiles while keeping a pensive eye on me. I realize it wasn't Death she was afraid of, but me! I was the unknown entity and Death was her friend and confidant.

She hugs him, grabs his hand, and begins walking in no particular direction. Death glances back at me and gives me a slight nod, and I become acutely aware that something important has been transferred through this exchange. Suddenly, I'm back at the dark fire circle, feeling my body against the cool earth, and I notice that I'm holding my breath.

I keep my eyes closed for several minutes, drinking in the conversations and messages I received in my out-of-body experience. This begins a six-month intensive connection with Grandfather Death, as I fondly call him, each time we connect through meditation, shamanic drumming, or Dreamtime.

## THE CEREMONY

The most important thing I learned from my encounters with Grandfather Death is that dying is not something that happens with our last breath. Its energy is with us our entire life, walking as close to us as our shadow, and we can learn to embrace the relationship, so when our final moment arrives, it's a deeply sacred journey with your best friend as your guide.

How can you accomplish this? It starts with paying attention to all the little deaths around you, recognizing death is part of a cycle that leads to life, possibility, and new beginnings.

This tends to be such a taboo subject in our western culture. It's no wonder we have trauma, avoidance, and fear around the concept of dying. There's even the belief everyone else is going to die but us, which keeps death at a distance. This doesn't give us any coping tools when it happens with family, friends, pets, illness, relationships, jobs, etc. These are the big deaths many of us encounter. When these arise, I invite you to pay attention to what gifts they offer, because there is always a gift, even if it doesn't seem like it in the moment.

I'm not trying to downplay the immense grief which accompanies these deaths, nor am I suggesting you avoid the grief and loss. On the contrary, I invite you to fully experience them, drinking deeply from what each has to offer while keeping your heart open and staying grounded through spiritual practices such as meditation.

Grandfather Death explained the importance of being present for the small deaths that happen daily. The transition from night to day and back again—each dying to the other. Paying attention when you go to bed each night and die to the conscious reality and enter the Dreamtime. The death of the seasons as they surrender to each other. Can you sense the exchange? Pay attention, and you will. The leaves change color and drop to the ground in fall. Plants release growth and production with winter's touch, and conversely, the reawakening of new life as spring coaxes plants from their temporary grave.

It's as important to pay attention to the small births as we do the small deaths, for they are part of the continuum and therefore, have important messages.

Many deaths occur in nature, but they also include projects ending, such as this chapter I'm writing, a Netflix series, books, movies, vacations, and other experiences we're invested in. There's a completion, a death, or a release, and the remaining void is an invitation for imagination and creation—birth.

Tibetan Buddhism places a particularly strong emphasis on instructions concerning death, and Tibetan literature is full of admonitions to be aware of the inevitability of death, the preciousness of the opportunities a human birth presents, and the great value of mindfulness of death.

The invitation is for you to be curious and open to all the deaths you encounter daily so you might begin your conversation with Death in whatever form it shows up. For me, it's a masculine grandfather figure, probably because of my culture and upbringing. Your relationship will likely be something completely different. Honor that, for Death shows up how you need it to, so you can recognize its deep love and support.

If you embark on this journey, you may find yourself looking forward to the small deaths, and the preciousness of life they offer, and perhaps, forge a deep companionship with Death, realizing you're never alone and can cross in a sacred way when your time comes, with your best friend as your guide and companion.

**Mark J. Platten** has his soul rooted in nature, in the holy and sacred communion with the earth and cosmos. His drive lies in helping people find their passion, purpose, and path by developing the integral human and connecting them with nature. He integrates brain science, rites/rituals/ceremonies, connection with nature, indigenous wisdom, and practical application in the physical realm to become the best version of ourselves.

He is the founder of Integral Human Initiative and Integral Man Institute and helps men and women align with their highest selves through Jungian archetypes, the four subtle bodies (physical, mental, emotional, and spiritual), and working with the subconscious to support our highest possibilities.

Mark's bestselling book, *The Art of Connecting With Nature,* is an anthology of 22 co-authors sharing how they connect with nature through various rites, rituals, ceremonies, and practices. You can find author interviews on his YouTube channel below and information about courses, rituals, and ceremonies on his website.

He is also a contributing author for three, number-one Amazon bestselling anthologies, and an international award-winning Haiku writer.

On the academic/professional side, Mark has an MBA in Organizational Management, served seven years as an Air Force officer, taught natural resources at the collegiate level, traveled internationally for 16 years as the lead environmental specialist for a company out of London, and since 2008, has been faculty at Colorado State University.

Connect with Mark:

Websites: www.markjplatten.com

Integral Human Initiative: www.integralhumaninitiative.com

Integral Man Institute www.integralmaninstitute.com

Facebook pages:
https://www.facebook.com/TheArtofConnectingWithNature
https://www.facebook.com/whennaturespeaks
https://www.facebook.com/IntegralManInstitute

YouTube for The Art of Connecting With Nature author interviews:
https://www.youtube.com/channel/UCQVjtyoGFr25I8xrz2dGQ8A

YouTube for Integral Man Institute:
https://www.youtube.com/channel/UCZ-eLsxRb8wAQ2FqfRO7t4g

You can contact Mark via email at markjplatten@gmail.com

# CHAPTER 22

# A RITE TO BREATHE

## CEREMONY AS A ROAD TO SOVEREIGNTY

Liz Goll Lerner, CAT, LCPAT, LPC, ATR-BC

## MY STORY

*Why Do It?*

*Rites and Rituals.*

Why do we mark any occasion?

So often we rush through life's most important moments. It's often easier to be out of the body or only in the head to avoid any sensory overload involved with the powerful moment we are committing to.

When we live the moment fully, and find a way to mark the occasion, we can feel ourselves propelled into a different position: Our next step.

For me, the process of divorce was different. The entire process was long, from knowing it was coming, to deciding the best way—including the best ways to behave, and the eventual separation and legal documentation.

I spent years living in and out of emotional reactivity—simultaneously recognizing the downfall of that for me, my child, and our family system. My former spouse and I made conscious decisions at various points in our son's life to stay together and create a safe and non-toxic environment. Our ability to be calm and collected was surely tested numerous times. It was by the grace of my training as a psychotherapist, my training as a spiritual teacher, and my own spiritual journey that I was able to use *all* the tools in my toolbox to create the template for the humane and often self-affirming divorce we eventually accomplished.

The vision had to be clear in order for all participants to make this happen—in our case the vision was keeping our son as healthy and unaffected as conceivably possible.

*Why Vision?*

*Vision: The Desired Outcome*

Vision is the ultimate key to all endeavors. Without vision the soul has no direction. Some might say without tuning into the soul's vision there is no true direction. No matter how you slice it, the key is to know what and why; when that is clear, the *how* follows swiftly and with ease if you're willing to trust your own heart. When you know what you truly want, miracles can happen.

When I came to the realization that our marriage had problems we couldn't solve, my child was two. *We really are operating out of completely different universes! I cannot believe we are talking about the same experience. It's as if we're in two different realities. How could we ever solve a problem if we're using differently perceived facts believed by each of us to be true?* It was a devastating realization. The dream of an uncomplicated, happy life was over. I knew my biggest support systems were out of state and I was afraid I couldn't make it on my own.

Fear is a big game changer because it can blind any of us to what is actually possible in life, which is why I work so hard to help my clients understand how to navigate it.

Our lifestyle was me staying home with our son and working minimally in my private practice. When I look back now, I see how fear blinded me, and I know it probably would've been okay, for all of us, had we parted at that moment in time.

But these decisions were complicated, and I wasn't ready to give up.

We each cherished our child and wanted to be parents—apparently together. We did love each other, but it took a tremendous amount of work and commitment to live together for 23 years. Our life was full of joys, sorrows, and challenges that come with a long life together. We separated when our son was a rising sophomore in high school. It was time. We prepared our son and ourselves, and then we did it swiftly. We continued the original vision. We kept the family intact in a different form. Was it challenging? Yes. Did it work? As best as it could.

The longevity, oddly, allowed us to work out many issues, so when we did eventually separate, we were able to work together for the good of us all.

The fact that we finally separated was hugely momentous. The idea that we were free and could go on with our lives was exciting. Challenges existed, as would be expected in any major change, especially while parenting and keeping a family construct alive. However, this was a change that was a long time coming and necessary. The return of psychic energy was immense. The freedom of no longer having to be super conscious of every word or action to keep the day-to-day status quo calm, peaceful, and respectful was a huge relief. No longer thinking: *Okay, he's got that tone, so I need to step back and assess what's happening here. How do I want to respond? Okay, I'm stepping back so I can be neutral and non-reactive—big breath. Move on. Protect the peace. Protect the child. Protect myself. This is not about winning; it is about strength, about my vision. No war.*

I noticed once we separated, I was caught by surprise when it became necessary to bring this self-discipline method back during various exchanges or the occasional family outing. It was an essential tool and one I was grateful to use much less frequently.

This was more than a moment in time. This was a cataclysmic shift in consciousness, life path, identity, and spirit. It was a rite of passage. The sadness as well as the excitement needed to be honored. The step off the cliff had to have wings!

# THE CEREMONY

*Rites of Passage:*

*My Ceremony*

Once the dust had settled on our new lifestyle it was time for me to say it out loud, as an individual, to the universe, and to myself, and to be witnessed and bear witness to the participants of the circle I gathered: My closest women friends.

As a family and couple, we already celebrated this change in our lives with a separation party. Not only did that mark the event and launch us on our new trajectories; it sent a clear message to our community that this divorce was different than what most were used to, and that we wanted their participation in helping that difference be supported with their behavior as well as ours.

The ceremony I created was different. It was about sovereignty, freedom, a right to breathe, and a right to be fully expressive of who I am. The right and honor to be present and witnessed were palpable, as it was to honor and witness the same in the women who gathered with me.

I led a three-part women's series for many years. Part two was called, *Creating Rites of Passage and Ritual.* I created it because so many women I knew, who joined the program, experienced events in their lives that were not greeting card moments or marked in any way in our culture, but were momentous and life-changing for them. These events needed a voice, and the women needed a way to mark them—body, mind, and spirit— as meaningful. Honoring and recognizing the journey that took place by doing and sharing was transformative.

Creating my ceremony was second nature. It was my turn.

Preparation:

1) The guest list

2) The invitation

3) The location

4) Sacred objects

5) The activity

6) The flow

7) The story

8) Closure

I chose to invite women from many different times in my life and my marriage—women I knew independently and women I knew as part of a couple. The women I invited were all quite different from each other. Some were into "woo-woo" consciousness, and some had never been to a women's gathering of any kind, seen an angel card, or thought about giving meaning to an object, etc. All of them, however, were there to support me marking this time in my life in whatever way I chose.

I went to a paper store and carefully chose beautiful purple card stock and envelopes and a shimmery pen, and with that act I began the journey of symbolic meaning. For me, beauty was key. I went home and decided on the space I'd use, the beautiful quilt that would demarcate the floor space we'd create our circle around. I chose the stones that would be placed around the circle. I chose the crystals, shells, and objet d'art that would adorn the space and which would be sacred objects in the center of our circle, heightened for our time together. I gathered a deck of symbolic cards each person would draw from. I set the scene focusing on natural elements and all elements that showed themselves to be important in all the rituals I attended and helped create. They included water for symbolic cleansing of the hands and heart, something wonderful to taste, which had meaning about the sweetness of life, sustenance, or nurturing. I included beautiful paper and writing implements so all could write something for themselves, as well as a message or a wish for me.

It's rare that we truly honor ourselves. It's even more unusual to allow or even ask others to acknowledge and honor us outside of traditional events like weddings, graduations, or religious rites of passage.

The time I spent being a wife, caring for in-laws and parents, being a mother, and growing my own internal and external garden was significant. I was ready and happy to honor all that took place. I was ready to fully greet the unknown.

I was still a mother and grateful for that gift. And I was ever changed—forged out of a myriad of experiences into a new and differently formed being. Maybe that's how I see and feel it now, but I know at the time, although a challenging road lay ahead, the strength and beauty of freedom, accomplishment, a job well done, and the right to breathe was at the fore.

And so, I set the circle with beautiful objects and a short itinerary at each place—a guide for the hour. I included instructions so all would know what to do and why. Everyone had a choice to participate or not. There was flow through each choice of stone, reading of a card, words spoken, written wishes, or the vocalizing of tones to bring us together to begin and to mark the end of our sacred time together.

I wanted the moments in this ritual/ceremony to make a time stamp in the universe—a marker of what was, what is, and the possibility of what was to come. That is the beauty of taking the action that brings you fully present and alert to the numinous moments in our lives.

There were some challenging twists and turns that occurred:

A latecomer affected our ability to begin, even though it was stated that time was sacred.

A strong personality trying to take over leadership of my carefully planned ceremony.

I surely couldn't have predicted such a disrespectful act, and it threw me off for a few moments. But what it taught me was that in spite of my carefully prescribed event, the universe was going to make me prove that I was indeed a sovereign being, that I was going to take the helm back and live my truth, that I wouldn't fall prey to the same behavior I was making ceremony to mark the end of. So, beware of the unexpected and rejoice in the testing of your mettle when you get thrown a curve ball.

*The Tool*

*Creating your own ceremony*

I think of a rite of passage as a singular event that has its own time and place and transports an individual from one state of being to another.

It's for you to decide the significant moments in your life and how you want to celebrate or mark them.

*Vision is your guide.*

Ask: What is compelling me to mark this moment in my life?

Write all the reasons.

Ask: What would I like to feel, see, and do to mark this occasion?

Write or draw your answers.

Ask: Do I want to do this alone or with others?

If with others, begin to think about who and make a list.

If alone, think about who, if anyone, you would like as a support person to assist in any way you might need.

Location: Inside or outside?

Now: Grab a journal or some paper, pencil, or markers to have by your side. Close your eyes and envision your ceremony taking shape. Allow yourself to imagine anything that would bring you joy. Imagine the elements that would feel exactly right to you. Direct the ideas of good or bad, right or wrong, can or can't, should or shouldn't, to take a vacation. With the caveat of doing no harm, creating the moment or ceremony that you feel with your entire being is what needs to be done.

To help get into visioning, you can use step one of my QPT™ (Quantum Presence technique) system. In a quiet place with head and heart connected, breath gently moving in and out, is a great place to start allowing yourself to touch into your wisdom.

Note: Some people are visual, and some are not. Some people are very tuned into the sensations of the body, and some are not. Any visualization instruction can be accomplished just as easily with your intention. All body sensation instruction can also be accomplished with your intention. In other words, don't get stuck on doing it right. Trust that you are.

Choose a place to begin that is private, feels safe, and where you will not be interrupted for about 15 to 20 minutes for your first attempt. In the future, you'll need much less time to successfully employ this technique, but guidance is critical during your first experience. In time, continued practice will help you access this technique in less time as you become more skillful.

*Find Your Feet*

The simplest way to get into your body—what many refer to as being grounded—is to find your feet and breathe. Your eyes can be open or closed. If closing your eyes creates a balance question, keep your eyes open with an unfocused gaze.

1. Stand (if able) or sit in a chair that supports your spine with your feet touching the floor.

2. Take a deep breath and put all your attention on the sensation of your feet connecting with the floor.

3. Focus your attention on the floor as it supports the weight of your body and breathe, putting all your attention into your feet. It's almost as if the breath is moving directly to your feet and all of your concentration is on what the bottom of your feet feel like as they are supported by the floor. Some of you may feel a tingling sensation, a heavy sensation, or a gluey sensation in your feet as you focus on connecting your feet to the floor. Extraneous thoughts may arise— simply return your attention to your feet.

4.  Now focus on your breath and breathe deeply, exhaling any stress that needs to be released.

5.  Remembering that gravity is connecting you to the Earth, imagine the beautiful Earth is sending you vital energy up through your feet and into your body. With every breath, that vital energy moves up your legs, into your torso, and into your arms, shoulders, neck, and head.

    Your body knows exactly what to do; you're simply taking a moment to become conscious of it. Every time you breathe, your body takes in nourishment, and lets go of what it doesn't need. Trust that is occurring. You are vitalizing every cell, muscle, tendon, and organ.

6.  Standing tall or seated in your chair, imagine a string connected to the top of your head gently pulling you into an upright (no slouch) position. Imagine breathing in through the top of your head, often referred to as the crown chakra. This will allow the energy to flow through you.

7.  Take a deep breath and put your hands on your heart—one on top of the other.

8.  Feel the sensation of the breath moving your chest.

9.  Visualize golden light in your chest/heart center and simply allow it to grow with every breath. Allow the golden light to move through your body, brightening every cell, muscle, tendon, and organ. Allow yourself to imagine your skin glowing with golden light.

10. Ask your heart—not your mind—*am I okay in this moment?*

The answer is *yes*.

If you've chosen a safe and quiet place to do this exercise, your body knows that you're safe at that moment, even if you might feel sad or have another emotion. You're physically okay. Our emotions often take us into fight or flight: an ancient reflex meant to protect us from harm. At this moment, there is no wooly mammoth or other immediate danger to your person. Your emotions are playing tricks on your mind. Trust your body.

How do I know I'm in my body? One sure way is to notice that thoughts aren't swirling, emotions aren't roiling; you are just standing, feeling your body, aware of your breath, feeling your feet connected to the floor, and that is all there is.

If you ask yourself if you're okay in this moment and the answer isn't *yes,* then your thoughts are continuing to distract you, feeding your emotions. Start again by breathing and putting all your attention on your feet.

This sense of being okay is an aspect of knowing, not of thinking.

Notice when you feel connected to your heart, and you feel a stillness. From this place, simply begin to understand the vision of what you want to achieve from doing a ceremony and write it down. Then, still being present and grounded, imagine what you'd like it to look like, feel like, smell like, taste like, and sound like, and who this time might be shared with.

Grab your journal, and you're on your way.

**Liz Goll Lerner** has over 40 years of experience as a coach, counselor, and art therapist. She is a spiritual teacher and communications expert. A true pioneer, she's developed many highly respected, groundbreaking psycho-educational and therapeutic programs for her own practice and for health centers across the nation. She was an adjunct professor at George Washington University and played a pivotal role in a longitudinal study focused on public health for the NIH through Georgetown University's Center on Health and Education.

With certifications in mindfulness practices, energy medicine, and bioenergetics, Liz uses multiple modalities in her integrative practice. Her unique approach is influenced by her deep understanding of the more subtle energies of the body and archetypal psychology. Above all, Liz is committed to creating an integrative, whole-system approach that helps her clients meet their full potential by connecting with their true purpose, putting that purpose into action, and healing blocks to growth. She is the creator of Divorce Well and Thrive®, The Healing Journey, The Women's Series, and she leads many other transformational retreats. Her most recent program, Enlightened Communication Through Luminous Living™, transforms the way individuals and organizations interact and communicate to help them achieve their goals in even the most high-stakes situations.

Connect with Liz:

For ways to go deeper, join me at:

Websites: https://Enlightenedcommunicationinstitute.com
https://yourinspiredchoices.com

Email: info@yourinspiredchoices.com

Chapter resource page:
https://yourinspiredchoices.lpages.co/rite-to-breathe/

# CHAPTER 23

# WHAT'S YOUR INTENTION?

## THE ART OF EVERYDAY CEREMONY

Jen Piceno, Prosperity Priestess, the Ceremonial Lifestyle Mentor

## MY STORY

I don't know about you, but I never skip my morning coffee.

Its earthy aroma fills the room, and I'm filled with joy as I breathe it in. It's a simple pleasure that simultaneously delights my senses, awakens my spirit, and amplifies high vibrations and contentment. The first cup is pure magic. It's filled with deep, robust intentions and charged with words that empower my day. Coffee becomes a ceremony, while sacred sips are intentionally anchored with purpose. My eyes close, and my awareness heightens—surrendering to the experience, my intentions absorb at a soul level, and I become an open channel to receive.

It's a burst of spiritual power, clarity, and divine success that an average cup of Joe simply cannot offer. It sets the tone of the day, my mood, and how I manifest everything on the spiritual plane.

As I fold my fingers around my favorite big red mug, the frequency of my intentions begins calibrating. Holding it with a tender embrace, sip by sip, my body feels lighter and lighter. I melt into the divine expression of compassion, love, and sacred serenity. It's delightful. Then, I listen carefully for divine wisdom. It gently pours through me as I enjoy my sacred sips.

*Call her,* the voice says.

*Call who?*

*Her.* An image of my client instantly flashes into my mind's eye with vibrant colors and a feeling of urgency.

Divine whispers and warmth move me into intentional action with clarity, one step at a time. There's a distinct knowing I feel on a physical level when messages are received from the divine. The "who" has already been revealed, but I'm not sure why I'm calling her. Zap! Autopilot ignites, and I'm guided to my notepad. I hear the words as they download from the divine through my hand and spill wildly onto the page. I scribe rapidly as it comes through, delighted by the sensation, power, and emotion it carries in each written word. I can hardly wait to deliver the message to her.

"Hello."

"Hi, Emma, it's Jen. I was guided to call you with a message this morning. Are you open to receiving what came through?"

Sobbing now comes from the other side of the phone, and I feel all her emotions aching deep in my heart. After a moment of silence, a crackling voice replies, "How did you know?"

I didn't know anything, but I trusted the divine guidance that this message was for her at this exact moment. I take a deep, grounding breath before reading the message to her. My body relaxes, and my guides tap me on the shoulder, and then I hear, *Now, dear.* So, I tell her, "This is what came through: Dear sister, no matter what is happening around you, you must remember who you are. You're a divine being in human form, and this is happening for you, not to you. What you're experiencing is a necessary initiation that will propel you forward beyond what your human mind can comprehend. You must trust in yourself and know you're being led. You're being asked to continue forward through the weight of this resistance. This message is to help you gain trust in yourself so you can dissolve self-doubt once and for all. You asked for a sign, and this is it. You're ready. The time is now."

I heard her gasp with a sharp inward breath, then exhale the weight of relief. She said, "I did. I asked for a sign last night." Weeping, she continued, "Thank you for this divine collaboration you have with Spirit.

I don't understand how you do what you do, but I'm grateful to have you in my corner. I know what I need to do now. I wouldn't have the courage without this call or without you. Thank you."

*"Little moments and acts of trust have a big impact."*

~ Jen Piceno

Everything is an invitation to a more profound life experience. Don't take anything for granted. Feel the air upon your skin on your morning walk or to the mailbox if that's as you make it! Hear the natural world speaking to you through the birds, flowers, and trees. We're surrounded by opportunities to make life filled with intentions and purpose.

...

The water is steaming hot, just as I like it. Scented rosebuds from my altar float above my toes. The aroma fills the bathroom, delighting my senses. I sink deeper into myself and the water. My eyes close, and I inhale a breath of gratitude for the air that enters my lungs with the essence of rose. Exhaling a sound of surrender, I'm more connected to my divine center and release the day. Embracing the sacredness I'm submerged in, my shoulders tingle and melt as I let go of stress from a busy day at my computer. Words emerge, and excitement builds as I hear *Alchemy Ceremonial Activation.* I'm intrigued and listening with heightened awareness. *90 minutes. It's your one-of-a-kind gift. A potent transformational blend of generational/ancestral healing, channeled transmissions, mediumship, energetic balancing, and light-codes activations.* My whole body tingles. *Two weeks of integration support.* I've never offered an extension to a single session. I love the idea and trust the overflowing excitement—it's a yes. *Today.* Today what? *Make the offer.* I agree without negotiating with my spirit guides. A checklist plays in my mind as I watch the water swirl down the drain, and with it, I send fears and doubts, conscious and unconscious. I gather the wet rose petals in my wrinkled, waterlogged fingers and gift them to the trees in my front yard as an offering of gratitude. Walking toward the house, the wind kisses my face. The leaves from the big oak reach out to caress my cheek. I hear, *Thank you, sister.* My heart expands, then my phone vibrates. Ana, a previous client, asks to work with me ASAP. I mention the Alchemy Ceremonial Activation.

"This is exactly what I need; send me the link." This is how we're led with divine inspiration.

You'll be asked to trust and deliver messages too. It won't always make logical sense, and the timing isn't always convenient. Trust that you're the messenger for a reason. You never know how or when you can change someone's life for the better, including your own.

...

I go about my day listening to the sound of crystal singing bowls vibrating through my body and home. I light candles and watch the flame dance in rhythm freely with my intentions. Incense burns, and the scent of copal billows into the air, inviting spiritual intelligence to fill my space. As I commune with my guides, the smoke carries my prayers to the heavens. My home is a sacred space, my temple.

Throughout the day, we're receivers of sacred instructions, purpose, and inspiration. Listen, and you'll hear wisdom in whispers of everyday moments. Feel the knowing stir in your chest and find answers to questions in the sounds of nature. It's simple yet powerful to live this way. Each thing we do and say adds layers of magic that activates intentions and our connection to the divine. The spiritual relationship that builds through simple everyday moments never ceases to amaze me.

As a priestess and energy medicine specialist, intentional living and ceremony are at the core of my teaching style and make me who I am. My style is rooted in Grandmother's medicine and woven with a modern shamanic twist. I've taken every experience, psychic gift, and initiation and seasoned it with a hand-crafted blend of soulful edginess and a healthy splash of magic. I'm a modern medicine woman who activates change and transformation in the lives of others and embodies its potent medicine at a cellular level. Intentions are everything to me.

Life becomes more and more beautiful as you discover who you are. It requires trust and a bit of creativity (word wizardry is fun). Play with it. The spiritual plane loves when we're passionate and playful with our intentions. The more you develop awareness, spiritual gifts, and abilities, the more you'll artfully embody lessons learned and get masterful glimpses of whom you're becoming next. It's a fascinating dance that works with us wherever we are in self-discovery. The ever-evolving relationship between all things seen and unseen is deep and wide.

**Relax, listen, feel, and trust you are being led; life will never be the same. Living in an everyday ceremony is an adventure of a lifetime!**

It's ecstatic when the art of creation can be seen with every interaction. Abundance and beauty are everywhere and in everything. Ceremony and ritual open us to a new lens of seeing the world. It's magical, mysterious, and filled with an abundant treasure of gems and jewels.

This art has worked magic in my life and continues to work through me, for me, and because of me in extraordinary ways with my clients, family, and friends. Experience it for yourself. It's ever-changing, deepening, widening, and expanding into fullness beyond my wildest imagination. It must be felt. It's the gift of prosperity in all forms.

My books *Sacred Medicine: Mystical Practices for Ecstatic Living* and *Wealth Codes: Sacred Strategies for Abundance* were created in sacred space and enchanted with intentions. I didn't write these books. They channeled through me with divine inspiration. Trust that your intentions matter and that your creations will knock your socks off. Everything is a ceremonial experience with a higher purpose.

Get started with simple ceremonies like putting love in the pot—it's everyday magic at its best. So is blowing out a birthday candle (or any candle) if your intentions are on point. Things don't have to be complicated to reap results. Intentionally directing energy and cultivating desires into form gets easier the more you practice. It's an art form that grows as you grow. You'll get better and better as you practice.

Start by layering energy with words, emotions, affirmations, and prayers into whatever you're cooking, eating, drinking, creating, and doing. It's transformational, fully expressed, creative, and has an ebb and flow, bringing ease and grace in with a potent dose of manifesting oomph. I'll take you into this experience, "Everyday Ceremony for Ecstatic Living," with a ritual below.

I'm sharing this simplicity with you because it changes everything. I mean, *everything*. When you recognize that it's the simplest things that ripple goddess-y goodness into our hearts, souls, and lives, you'll move throughout the day from sacred sips to intentional everything.

It keeps divine inspiration moving through us, and we become sacred vessels for divine intelligence. Who wouldn't want to start their day like that? Hell, who wouldn't want to live their life like that?

This lifestyle gives purpose to everything. It's simple, powerful, and sacred. I layer magic upon magic and make the experience as simple or complex as I'm guided to do, say, and experience. As a priestess and accomplished ceremonialist, it's an honor to guide people through life and business enrichment in this way. This is how I coach, mentor, and hold space for healing anyone I have the pleasure of working with.

With each year that passes, I embody these teachings more deeply to expand the context into living my legacy now, and I teach others to do the same. It flows into wealth, leadership, parenting, human potential, sisterhood, art, relationships, businesses, and everything else. You'll hear me share my passion for this on The Ecstatic Living Podcast, Mystic Circle, my complimentary Facebook community for women, and my online academy.

I'm ever-evolving, just like you. Let's dance and co-create through the art of ceremony. It's a magical journey. Join me. It's easy to live this way once you get the hang of it. There's nothing quite like it, either. All senses wake up and proclaim, *Yes, this is living*. Gratitude and appreciation for minor things will radiate in your heart, and the experience of simply being you will become richer.

We live in an enchanted land with the art of ceremony at our fingertips. The elements in the natural world (earth, water, fire, air, and Spirit) invite us to remember who we are so we can connect deeply with all things. There was a time when everything was sacred, and through simple practices, we can make it so again. Waking up our most magical selves is an adventure into our greatest human potential. That excites me because it's an experience drenched in sacred beauty and aligned with divine purpose. If you're intrigued, come with me on this journey into self-expansion. It starts by saying yes to yourself, saying yes to living on your own terms, and saying yes to ecstatic living.

We are the elements, and the sacred power they hold lives within us. In ceremony, what was once dormant becomes aroused and alive with passion and purpose. The ordinary human experience is a landscape in which we plant seeds of intentions. Then, the ordinary becomes extraordinary. We co-create with the universe, and our intentions grow into better-than-expected outcomes with sacred purpose.

I'm inviting you to harness this art form in the simplest habits and routines you already have. All you have to do is be present, intentional, and heart-centered. If you do, life will become more magical right before your eyes. Things will become apparent and vibrant, and what was once mundane will become magical, sacred, and rich.

# THE CEREMONY

## EVERYDAY CEREMONY FOR ECSTATIC LIVING

Take a deep breath in and know you are a divine being in human form. Ceremony is a practice, an art form that will evolve as you evolve. Be playful and creative or straightforward and to the point, but always be intentional and savor the experience. This is an invitation to ecstatic living.

This is where you get to take what you've read and implement it into your life. It's the best part!

You're about to see how easy it is to take any habit or routine you're already doing and transform it into a ceremony.

By choosing routines and habits, we aren't taking any extra time out of your already busy day. Mundane moments will become magical richer life experiences. And you get to step into life seeing things differently.

Here are a few examples of things that can be easily made into ceremonial experiences:

- Brushing your teeth
- Bathing/showering
- Drinking coffee/tea
- Cooking
- Cleaning the house
- Doing yardwork
- Putting on makeup
- Lighting candles

- Paying bills
- Receiving money
- Watering plants
- Exercising

Pretty basic stuff, right? I know. That's what's so awesome about living intentionally. The most basic tasks become a vehicle for divine intervention. The most mundane tasks become enjoyable, magical, and soul-aligned by speaking words of prayer, affirmation, and intention into our actions and trusting the art of ceremony itself. Life becomes more vibrant and joyful.

Sparks of inspiration (or downloads) come pouring in and life's purpose for the day becomes more apparent. Knowing stirs in our hearts, and the sensations of our gifts can shine.

It doesn't have to be challenging, but it must be intentional.

But how, you ask?

### K.I.S.S. (Keep it simple and sacred)

The journey of expansion is rich with ritual and ceremony. Allow yourself to dance with it. Let the energy move you. The power and sensations come in with distinct characteristics, wisdom, and emotions. Each ceremony, ritual, and tradition have a personality and purpose. Allow yourself to be led, and you will be.

The art of ceremony is part of our divine blueprint. It's filled with sensations, wisdom, and heart-opening ah-has. Trust the journey and savor the moment.

## COFFEE/TEA/CACAO RITUAL

My personal favorites for enhancing sacred sips and practices can be found at https://www.jenpiceno.com/shop. You'll see organic teas, herbs, cacao, and protein shakes (I'm a foodie and love delicious things). Get the ceremonial cacao for opening your heart! There's a complimentary cacao ritual and a recipe for that at www.jenpiceno.com/resources too.

Step 1: Choose your favorite mug.

Step 2: Hold it in your hands and bless the mug with your purest intention by saying, "This is now a sacred object for divine guidance."

Step 3: Pour your drink into the cup and place your hands above the steamy liquid in the shape of a triangle (the alchemy symbol for fire) representing the transformation symbol.

Step 4: Speak your intentions. This can be an affirmation, mantra, prayer, incantation, or word of the day. This is an affirmation I wrote to call in sacred wealth: "Divine compensation comes to me from multiple sources, easily, soulfully, joyfully, and in expansive increments with integrity and great purpose."

Step 5: Affirm that you trust it is already happening. You can do this by saying, "And so it is," with gratitude and appreciation.

Step 6: The liquid in your mug is now blessed and charged with your intentions. Each sip now becomes sacred. Drink the words into your body, absorbing the frequency and high vibrations.

Step 7: Be aware of thoughts, feelings, or emotions that stir. Make a note in your journal and move through your day with sacred purpose. The same intentions can be used for any other routine or habit, which keeps the energy and intention in motion and makes life a living ceremony. The universe will respond accordingly.

Step 8: Gratitude, gratitude, gratitude.

The Ceremonial Alchemy Activations mentioned in my story and other experiences can be scheduled here: https://jenpiceno.com/book_now/

Delve into prosperity consciousness with The Sacred Wealth Masterclass. It's available as a complimentary offering for a limited time at: https://jen-s-school-01e8.thinkific.com/courses/the-sacred-wealth-masterclass

Other resources to ease you into the magical path and assist you with your spiritual journey through the art of ceremony are available at www.jenpiceno.com/resources

Weave wealth into all areas of life (money, relationships, freedom, vitality, and spirituality) with a ritual for each in *Wealth Codes, Sacred Strategies for Abundance*. On Amazon here: https://amzn.to/3CtoECt

Stay connected or learn more with my quick links: www.jenpiceno.com/links

**Jen Piceno,** Prosperity Priestess, Sacred Wealth Activist, Master Ceremonialist ORDM, RTM, MT, THP.

Begin the transformation you've been craving and live your legacy now. Jen is an energy medicine practitioner and modern medicine woman with 30+ years of experience in the healing arts. She'll help you bust through limitations to solidify your purpose and make sure you have fun doing it.

Align with everything you were meant to be in ways you've never experienced. Jen takes clients on an epic ceremonial adventure that crushes time and limitations. Then, she welcomes you into an ecstatic life without sacrificing joy, success, passion, or pleasure.

Jen is a bestselling author of *Sacred Medicine: Mystical Practices for Ecstatic Living,* author of *Wealth Codes: Sacred Strategies for Abundance,* and the host of The Ecstatic Living Podcast. She's a motivational speaker, coach, transformational teacher, ghostwriter, and a passionate woman savoring life and teaching others to do the same. Jen graced the stage as a professional salsa dancer, trained as an athletic competitor, and is a lifetime student of human potential and mystical practices.

She's on a mission to create worldwide holistic wealth, prosperity, and happiness in homes, lives, and businesses. She works with celebrities, athletes, high achievers, and women starting new phases of life. She's sought after as an innovator of change, transformation, passion, and purpose.

To work with Jen, schedule a discovery call at: www.jenpiceno.com/book_now

Checkout The Ecstatic Living Podcast at: https://open.spotify.com/show/67H5QDKCfb8u3QWOKdHzKS? si=90076a8967d24d3d

Visit her online academy at www.jenpiceno.com/academy

Join Mystic Circle, her online community for women, at: www.facebook.com/groups/jenpicneo

Visit: www.JenPiceno.com or get access to all quick links here: www.jenpiceno.com/links

# CLOSING WORDS

As Rumi says, "Don't go back to sleep."

Reading this book may have awakened something inside you that was lying dormant. If so, take a little time for mindful awareness.

On any given day, you might find yourself in a new place. When you cross a threshold into a room you've never entered before, you pause to get your bearings. Where's the light switch? What furniture is present? Is there anyone in the room with you?

In the spiritual world, it's much the same. As you stand at this threshold of awareness, notice what's shifted. What did you learn? Does anything inside you need attention? Perhaps a story stirred something up, or your soul is calling to know more about a particular rite or ritual that was shared. How would you like to move forward?

Should you wish to cross the threshold into deeper understanding, I encourage you to do so. Please join us in our facebook group at https://www.facebook.com/groups/ritesandrituals

This group is a great place to access all the authors, learn more about rites and rituals, and share your experiences.

If this book has awakened a calling in you and you are interested in becoming certified as a ceremonialist, please visit my website at www.asoulfullworld.com/masterceremonialist for information about training.

As you set out on the path ahead, know this—YOU are the spiritual authority in your life. If you want the world to improve, begin with simple steps to improve your life. The whole universe is waiting to co-create with you.

I invite you to complete this experience by writing a few words in a journal if you have one. When that's done, thank the teachers, ancestors, and guides who were present to support you. Then, if you lit one, blow out the candle and take a few cleansing breaths to release this experience.

Be sure to gift *yourself* with a moment of gratitude for your courage and willingness to explore something new. An "attitude of gratitude changes everything," my teachers tell me. I'm good at being grateful for everything except myself. I often forget to be grateful for me. How about you?

*Live Soulfully!*

*Ahriana*

# ABOUT THE LEAD AUTHOR

## REV. DR. AHRIANA PLATTEN

Ahriana's professional background is quite unique. For more than thirty years, she has led a bivocational life, spending half her time as an entrepreneur and business consultant, and half her time in spiritual leadership. She's led international research and strategic development teams in North American, South America, Asia, Africa, Europe, and the Middle East.

Ahriana is the founder of asoulfullworld.com, a global wisdom community, where she helps people master the art of living an authentic, purpose-driven, passionate life. Often referred to as a wisdom keeper, a practical mystic, and a leading-edge coach for visionaries, influencers, entrepreneurs and spiritual leaders, Ahriana believes there is nothing more vital than creating a meaningful life and having real impact on the world, and she loves to provide tips and tools for discovering your sacred calling.

A former Ambassador for the Parliament of the World's Religions, Ahriana is featured in the acclaimed international docuseries, "Time of the Sixth Sun." She's traveled the world to explore its cultural differences and human similarities, speaking to religious and indigenous leaders from over 250 tribes and traditions, and her interfaith column is read by 30,000 people a week.

With more than 30 years of metaphysical training, Ahriana is a certified Transpersonal Hypnotherapist, an ordained Unity Minister, a Reiki Master/ Teacher in the Usui lineage, a 3rd degree High Priestess in two esoteric religious traditions and has studied with indigenous teachers and medicine people. Her doctoral focus on Pastoral Counseling Psychology supports her bridge building efforts.

Ahriana lives from a blend of Eastern and Western ideologies that include the concepts of universal consciousness, interconnection, and relational accountability. She currently serves as a US liaison for Feed14K, a nonprofit organization addressing food scarcity in South Africa, and she is the board president of Citizens-Powered Media.

Contact Ahriana -

- For Certified Ceremonialist Training
- When you're ready to grow your spiritual, holistic, or purpose-driven business
- To receive daily Inspirations, blogs, podcasts

Connect with Ahriana:

Through her website: www.asoulfullworld.com.

In the Rites and Rituals Facebook Group: https://www.facebook.com/groups/ritesandrituals

On her Facebook page: https://www.facebook.com/ahriana.platten

On Instagram: https://www.instagram.com/ahriana_platten/

Or by email at Ahriana@asoulfullworld.com

*A portion of the proceeds from this book will support Feed14K.

# Products & Resources

## THE CHANGING STORY

A gift book for children and people
of all ages
Written by Ahriana Platten,
Illustrated by April Lavely-
Robinson
Winner of the Coalition of
Visionary Resources Silver Award
in Children's Books

**asoulfullworld.com/
changingstory**

*Amazon
Best Seller!*

## Get your free resource:

### 30 DAYS OF SIMPLE CEREMONIES

A free 30-day series of simple
ceremonies you can incorporate
into your everyday life.

**asoulfullworld.com/
simpleceremonies**

## BUSINESS MASTERMIND FOR HEALERS, INTUITIVES, AND SPIRITUAL EDUCATORS

If your spiritual or personal
development business is under-
performing, Ahriana's Inner Circle
Business Mastermind will help you
figure out why--and fix it:

**asoulfullworld.com
/innercircle**

## MASTER CEREMONIALIST CERTIFICATION PROGRAM

A 12-month immersion in the
sacred art of ceremony. Delve
deep into every aspect of the
creation, implementation, and
post-ceremony completion of rites
and rituals. Classes available for
novices to experienced spiritual
leaders.

**masterceremonialist.com**

# Become a Certified *master* Ceremonialist

Transform your ceremonial practices to a higher level, grow your business sustainably, and make a lasting difference in the lives of those you serve.

The Soul-full World Master Ceremonialist Certification program is the opportunity you've been searching for to grow your ceremonial understanding, relevance, and practice in spirituality and business.

Over our 12 months together, you will learn to facilitate more than a dozen different ceremonies, the ethics of ceremonial business, how to create sacred space and life-changing transformation, and how to create a sustainable business model offering your services as a Master Ceremonialist.

Let us support you in your ceremonial practice so you can thrive and prosper as you serve!

**LEARN MORE & APPLY:**

**masterceremonialist.com**

★★★★★

"I highly recommend this program with Rev. Ahriana. Although I'm a seasoned officiant, this has brought new insight and inspiration to my practices. I feel expansive and inventive about holding sacred space at the threshold of many of life's transitions."

*Rev. Mary Love*

★★★★★

"Minister or not, this program offers a deeper sense of understanding, mindfulness, harmony, relevance, and reverence to any gathering or ceremony going forward. Dr. Ahriana Platten is a master ceremonialist in transforming hearts and minds."

*Donna K. Grant*

★★★★★

"This program is so unique and needed for bringing the sacred into daily life to a broader audience. Thank you so much for the inspiration, creative and 'holy' options!"

*Rev. Marcia Beachy*

## LEARN MORE & APPLY:

masterceremonialist.com

## Your job is to inspire & nourish others but who inspires **you**?

At A Soul-full World, we provide affordable programs and coaching to support spiritual healers, teachers, and guides to grow thriving businesses that nourish both you *and* those you serve.

### JOIN THE INNER CIRCLE MASTERMIND:

asoulfullworld.com/innercircle

Printed in Great Britain
by Amazon

41431003R00139

# RITES
## and
# RITUALS

## HARNESSING THE POWER
## OF SACRED CEREMONY

# AHRIANA PLATTEN, PH.D

FEATURING: REV. ASHERAH ALLEN, DR. AVEEN BANICH,
ROGER BUTTS, MAEVEN ELLER-FIVE, LIZ GOLL LERNER, TINA GREEN,
ERICA JONES, JANA ROSELYNN LAIRD, REV. SHENNA LEE-BELMORE,
REV. MARY ROSE LOVE, KELLI MURBACH, JEN PICENO,
REV. MARK J. PLATTEN, JANICE PRATT, MILAGROS RUIZ BELLO,
MISTY DAWN SHAKTI SHARMA, HEATHER SOUTHARD,
KAT SPARKS, SUSAN M THOMPSON, REV. JESSICA TROVIK